learning to walk

*Taking baby steps
to Christian maturity*

DR. RICK CHESHER

Learning to Walk

Copyright © 2022 by Dr. Rick Chesher. All rights reserved.

No part of this publication may be reproduced, stored in a retrieval system or transmitted in any way by any means, electronic, mechanical, photocopy, recording or otherwise without the prior permission of the author except as provided by USA copyright law.

The opinions expressed by the author are not necessarily those of URLink Print and Media.

1603 Capitol Ave., Suite 310 Cheyenne, Wyoming USA 82001
1-888-980-6523 | admin@urlinkpublishing.com

URLink Print and Media is committed to excellence in the publishing industry.

Book design copyright © 2022 by URLink Print and Media. All rights reserved.

Published in the United States of America

Library of Congress Control Number: 2021924980
ISBN 978-1-68486-056-2 (Paperback)
ISBN 978-1-68486-057-9 (Digital)

23.11.21

INTRODUCTION

The purpose of this book is to show new Christians, and older Christians the importance of growth in the Lord. One can be saved and never take the next step in the process of their Christian walk. And often times, we as older Christians think that as long as we are going to church, that is all that is needed.

Unfortunately, this is an all too often occurrence within the walls of the church today. We are giving birth to new babies and leaving them to fend for themselves. This world is a pretty scary place when you have no idea where to turn, and what to do. Many of these Christians just fall away, and we never see them again. And many times if we do see them again, they have grown so cold that they don't want to hear what you have to say.

All of us have heard them talk. It goes something like this, I have tried religion, and it just didn't work for me. I just didn't find what I needed and so it became a waste of my time. Unfortunately, that is our fault, to some extent. They do have a responsibility for themselves, but we have a responsibility to them. Our responsibility is to teach them in the ways of the Lord.

The Great Commission says more than we are to go out and lead people to Jesus. It also says that we are to teach these new disciples the things that Jesus had commanded us to do. So every person that is brought to Christ has a responsibility of their own, but we as mature Christians have a responsibility to them that comes from a commandment given to us by Jesus Himself.

None of us would even think about parenting a baby, and once the baby was born, just leaving that baby on the sidewalk some where, and saying, Okay, your born, now get up and do the things necessary to make a living and fend for yourself. Even our secular laws have things to say about that. If someone did that the laws would have them thrown in jail, and they would go about to give them the longest sentence they could come up with.

If you were honest with yourselves, you would most likely be among those that were saying," throw the book at them; they don't deserve to ever see the light of day". But at the same time, are you doing that to new Christians? You may say, oh, that is not the same; this world can be a horrible place for a baby. Your right! It can be a horrible place for a baby.

This world can be a horrible place for the new Christian as well. The things that the new Christian faces, in the spiritual realm are things that they are not able to understand, and Satan will devour them. The Bible tells us that the Devil is like a lion that is moving back and forth, looking for whom to devour.

The truth of the matter is, if your have ever watched the nature shows on T.V. you have seen lions looking for their next meal. When they are looking, they are not looking for the fastest, and strongest of the herd. They are looking for the weak, which is usually the young, the sick, and the slowest.

If Satan is looking for someone to devour, who do you expect He will look for? He will look for the ones that are not living the Christian lives that they ought to be living. Who do you think that might be? Of course, it is those that choose disobedience, and those that don't know any different. Those that have come to the Lord, and don't know what to do next are the ones that are the most likely to be in Satan's sights.

It is our job to take our young and begin to bring them up in the Lord, and surround them so they are protected. Then they are under the covering of the church and we are protecting them from the attacks that are going to come. We are to build relationships with them so they will trust us and come to us as well.

The reason I am writing this book is for the new Christian. It is to show them the things that are important for their growth in the Lord. The things that will protect them from the attacks that Satan will level against them. But it is also for the mature Christians, who have been in the church for a while, and knows the wiles of the Devil. This is so they can understand the importance of taking the young Christian under their wing and teaching them to be mature Christians.

This book is really a guide to discipleship, both to the new Christian and to the mature Christian. This is a guide to help both know the things they must know to survive the spiritual warfare of our times, and not only survive, but also to grow and prosper in the faith.

Hopefully this book will help the church recognize their responsibility in the rearing of their young. We need them strong in the faith, so they too can be the warriors that we need in today's church. The time is short, and we have a great responsibility to the world around us. But most of all, we have a great responsibility to our Lord and Savior Jesus Christ.

CHAPTER 1

Bible Knowledge

It is vitally important, and I think that most would agree, that the new baby Christian learn the Word of God. One might say, that this goes without saying. The trouble is that in the church today, one of the things that, continually, become more and more apparent to me, is the lack of the knowledge of the Bible.

People in the church today don't know what God's Word has to say about the situations that they are faced with on a daily basis. This brings up a vital question, how do the people live the Christian life, in the world we live in? The answer is they don't. They have the world so intertwined in their lives that it is difficult to tell them from the world.

Today's church has a little of Christianity, world philosophy, and new age fixed together in their lives, and they are complaining that the Christian life doesn't work, and they are pouring into pastor's offices and telling pastor's that they have tried this and that and it is not working. Others are taking parts of the Bible, the part they are comfortable with, and only applying those parts. This is called denying the power of the Gospel.

The truth of the matter is this. When the church is not founded on Jesus Christ, and the building on the foundations is not God's Word, the building is going to collapse. Paul talks about this in 1 Cor. 3:10-15, "According to God's grace that was given to me, as a skilled master builder I have laid a foundation, and another builds on it. But each one must be careful how he builds on it, because no one can lay any other foundation than what has been laid-that is, Jesus Christ. If anyone builds on the foundation with gold, silver, costly stones, wood, hay, or straw, each man's work will become obvious, for the day will disclose it, because it will be revealed by fire; the fire will test the quality of each one's work. If anyone's work that has built survives, he will receive a reward. If anyone's work is burned up, it will be lost, but he will be saved; yet it will be like an escape through fire."

What is being said here is this, the only foundation that anyone can have and be stable in this life is Jesus Christ. He needs to be the very core of our lives. When life storms come He is the one that we turn to. But, we need to take it farther from there. Everything that we build on that foundation must be the truth for life, and that can only come from the Word of God.

Paul uses gold, silver, and costly stones here to represent the Word of God. If we were to look at these things we would find that the way they are purified is through fire or heat. Gold and silver are melted in a melting pot, so hot that they become liquid. What this does is it brings the impurities to the surface of the gold, or silver, so that the impurities can be removed from the surface of the gold or silver. The result is that the gold and silver become even more pure than they were before.

Interestingly enough, the things that Paul describes as falsehood, or false doctrine are hay, wood, and straw. Interestingly enough, these things are usually the things that are the impurities in the gold or the silver, and are the things that come to surface, or are burned away from the gold or silver.

The wood, hay, and straw are the world philosophy, the new age ideals, and the world's way of doing things. These are the things that Paul says needs to be removed from our lives. In fact, these are the things that Paul says ought not to be built into our lives. But Paul goes on to say, that at some point in our lives they will be removed. It could be at Judgment day, but it could be as we live our lives.

Peter talks about this in 1 Peter 1:6-7, "You rejoice in this, though now for a short for a short time you have had to be distressed by various trails so that the genuineness of your faith- more valuable than gold, which perishes though refined by fire- may result in praise, glory, and honor at the revelation of Jesus Christ."

Peter is saying that God considers our faith in Him to be more valuable than gold, and He will do what it takes to make our faith in Him more pure. And once again we see that the refining of gold is used to represent our faith in Him. Peter says that gold is refined by fire. Fire melts the gold and all of the impurities come to the surface so they can be removed, leaving only the gold.

Peter is teaching that the trials, and the tribulations that we go through in this life are for the purpose of refining our faith. They turn up the heat on our lives, and what comes to the surface are the things that need to be removed. The false doctrines, the world's ways, the new age thoughts, everything that is not from Him comes to the surface. The reason is that He wants to makes us more like His Son, Jesus Christ. He refines us in this manner, so that we can be transformed into the image of Jesus Christ.

This is a must to know if we are going to disciple the new baby Christians that are being born into our midst. We have to know it first for us, so we aren't caught by surprise, and we must be able to teach them what they will be experiencing, and let them know this is a natural process.

When I first became a Christian, I went through this, as will all new Christians, they may have a period of time that is pure bliss, but the trials will come. When I went through these times, no one told me about God using these things to build my faith. They just tried to minister to the specific need.

The trouble with this is, they may go through a series of trials, and it may seem that they are never going to come out of these trials. My thought was there is no way I am going to make it. I thought that all of this stuff would stop because I had been healed and delivered from all of this.

Had someone come along and told me that these things are normal, and are God's way of purifying me and building my faith in Him, I would have looked at things a little bit different. When I got saved, everyone that was involved was rejoicing, and so they ought to be. But no one told me there would be things to face down the road, and no one said these things would make you better. In fact, everyone looked just as baffled as I did.

No one took me to God's Word, specifically 1 Peter 1:6-7, and had me look at these things. I'm not even sure they knew about these things and what the Word of God says about these things. No one explained to me just what God was doing. I ended up finding these things on my own later. Thank God for His mercy and His grace, and His ability to hold us through it all.

People that come to Christ, and ask Him to be their Lord and Master need to know what God's Word says about their life. Not just how to be saved, but how to live, how it all applied to their lives, and the choices they need to make for the result God wants in their lives. This is our responsibility to these new Christians. We can't just say to them, well, you are a new creation in Christ, now go out and live like it, and leave them to the wolves. The wolves will devour them, and we will be discouraged as to why these people aren't staying.

It is true that they have a responsibility in their growing process. And they have to make the decision to stay put, and endure to the ended. But if we don't teach them about what to expect, according to God's Word, they will get blind sided by the wiles of the Devil, and become causalities of war. Unfortunately, the next thing they do is to become discouraged, decide that it isn't working and drop out of church all together.

How we minister to others:

One of the things that I hear all of the time from people in the church is, I don't know how to minister to people. I haven't really done any of the stuff that some of these others have done. It's kind of like saying that I really haven't been a sinner, so I don't know how to minister to sinners.

This to me is somewhat of a problem for these people. They don't seem to realize that it really doesn't matter if they had done the same things that I have done, we were all going to hell, had it not been for Jesus Christ, and the work He did of the cross. It is His blood that made it possible for me to be righteous, and the same is true for all of us.

This is a key point. Jesus made it possible for all of to experience the mercy and grace that God has extended to us. He made it possible for all of us to come into an intimate relationship with Him. If it were not for Him, all of us would be searching, and unable to find peace with God, and with one another.

It says in 2 Cor. 1:3-7, "Blessed be the God and Father of our Lord Jesus Christ, the Father of mercies and the God of all comfort. He comforts us in all our afflictions, so that we may be able to comfort those who are in any kind of affliction, through the comfort we ourselves receive from God. For as the sufferings of Christ overflow to us, so our comfort overflows through Christ. If we are afflicted, it is for your comfort and salvation; if we are comforted, it is for your comfort, which is experienced in the endurance of the same sufferings that we suffer. And our hope for you is firm, because we know that as you share in the sufferings, so you will share in the comfort."

Look at what is being said here. Verse 3 says that the Father is the God of all mercies and comfort. All that go through any suffering, in the Lord, will find mercy and comfort from the Father. Have you been through the sufferings of this Life? If so, what happened? How did God comfort you through all of that? They way that God gave you relief is important for you to think about.

Now, look at verse 4. Paul says that God does comfort us. Sometimes we just don't look at it as being from God. We may have seen Susan, or Bill, or anyone else that came along side of us. We thanked them for their support and their willingness to go through these things with us. But in reality it was the Father of all comfort. You came into contact with God and learned God in a different way.

Let's finish verse 4. The reason that God comforted you was not jus to comfort you, even though His desire was to comfort you, but it was also to teach you to comfort others who are suffering the same way that He comforted you. And Paul goes on to say that they had been afflicted for them. He is talking about the lessons that they learned from the sufferings that they went through.

Paul was able to comfort them in their afflictions, because Paul knew the suffering of affliction. Paul knew every aspect of suffering. He knew the temptation to become discouraged, and he explains that in verses 8-10 of chapter 1. He knew the beginning from the end in suffering. He may not have known the specific kind of suffering, but he did know what experiences sufferings bring.

I may not know what it is like to face an abortion for instance, but what I do know is what it is like to face uncertain times. A woman who has become pregnant out of wedlock, and is not employed, and has no family to be able to turn to, certainly faces uncertain times. In fact her whole life at that moment may seem to have come to a dead end with no way to escape, it seems, outside of that abortion. That may seem the only way out for her at the time. She may even hate the idea of having that abortion, but may see no other option in her life at the time.

I don't know what it is like to be pregnant, but I do know what it is like to have no way out. I have faced times when I didn't think I had any place that I could turn. No one was there to talk to, no one was there to listen to the way that I was feeling, and no one was there to walk through the situation with me.

I felt that my life was over. All things seem to point to only one way and it wasn't a good option, but it seemed the only one I had. I know the pressure that I felt to make some kind of a decision. I know the agony I felt as I approached that decision. I know the depression that I felt, because I knew the out come of the decision that I was about to make, but I saw no other option.

I don't have to know what it is like to be pregnant out of wedlock with no options, but I do know what emotional state that person may be in. And that is what I can address, because I know how God met me in that situation. I know how God sent comfort to me as I felt the way that I did. And that is what you can do as well.

You can also tell them what God is doing by sharing these verses with them. This will not only help comfort them, but it will also teach them the Word of God and how it applies to your life. You are teaching them God's Word, and showing them what it looks like, all at the same time. This is how it is suppose to work!

The Old Gone:

The other thing that I have seen happen is, that the new Christian comes under the scrutiny of the church, or those that happen to know them before they were saved. Paul says in 2 Cor. 5:17, "Therefore if anyone is in Christ, there is a new creation; old things have passed away, and look, new things have come."

This is to be taken just like that, old things are dead, and they were buried with Christ.

Paul said in Verse 16, "From now on, then, we do not know anyone in a purely human way. Even if we have known Christ in a purely human way, yet now we no longer know Him like that." Paul is saying that once a person turns to Christ, and they have become a new creation in Him, he quits looking at them according to the flesh, and their past. He starts looking at them according to the spirit. He means that he begins to look at the spiritual fruit that is produced in their lives, a little at first, then more and more as they grow.

God says that when we come to Him and ask for forgiveness, He chooses to remember our sins no longer. If He doesn't remember our sins, what right do we have to remember their sins? Then it becomes our sin, and it is us who need to repent. No only that instead of being an encouragement to these new Christian, we keep their sins before them and we become a discouragement. Remember what Jesus said about being a stumbling block to the little ones, and the new Christian is a little one.

They are brought into the Kingdom of God by God, they are placed in the body where God has put them, who are we to argue with God, but yet that is exacting what we are doing when we continue to look at them according to the flesh. We have gone back to the tomb, and we have drug the old dead person out of the grave, and we have tied the dead man to them for them to carry around.

We are there to teach them, to encourage them in the faith, not to remind them of their past, they will do enough of that on their own. In fact, we are suppose to remind them that the old man is dead, and they need to start looking at themselves as the new man that God created. We need to remind them that God has forgiven them, and they need to forgive themselves as well.

Faith:

The walk we walk, or the life we live, as a Christian is one of faith. In fact, 2 Cor. 5:7 says, "For we walk by faith, not by sight". And this is something that every Christian, that has been a Christian for any length of time, has heard this Scripture quoted to them a least once in their lifetime. When we go to talk to someone during a trying time in our lives, we are reminded that, "we walk by faith, not by sight". And this is true, and we need to pay attention to this.

The truth of the matter is, if we were really honest with ourselves and those around us this is much easier to say than to do, especially if it has been a long trail that we are experiencing. But, we continue to believe, or shall we say, we choose to believe that God will take us through and protect us.

The question must be asked at this point, why are we choosing to believe that God will take us through all of the things that we are experiencing? Do we just believe this to make ourselves feel better, kind of a mental pump up? Or psyching ourselves up so we are able to make it through?

No! We are choosing to believe what the Word of God says about our situation, and our relationship with a living God. This is what it says in the Bible, Romans 10:17, "So faith comes from what is heard, and what is heard comes through the message about Christ." This is what the Word of God says about our situation. This is God speaking to us through His Word, and He is speaking to our situation.

By listening to what He says in His Word, and by choosing to believe it, we then put it into practice in our lives, and we begin to live out the Word of God. We are then walking by faith, and being pleasing to God. And as we are faithful in our walk with Him, He rewards us by delivering us through the situation, and our faith becomes stronger.

Not only is it important to live by faith, not living by faith can cause a complete brake down of our relationship with the Lord. In Romans 14:23 it says, "But whoever doubts stands condemned if he eats, because his eating is not from faith, and everything that is not from faith is sin."

Now get this, and listen to this very carefully. Some would say that Paul is talking about eating here, and he is, but think this out. If not having faith in what we eat is important, how much more in all we do in this life that has been given to us from God through Jesus?

It says here that anything that is done, that is done without faith is a sin. So think about this for a moment, if we are living our lives in such a way that it isn't faith in the Lord Jesus, we are living in sin, and if we are living in sin, then our fellowship with Him is broken, and we are not hearing clearly from Him. And if we are not hearing clearly from Him, then some of the things we are doing may be in the flesh and not His will for our lives.

What an impact that would have to our daily living, or would it? With some they are so used to living like this that they don't know the difference. They think they are doing just fine, when in reality they are doing things on their own. This would explain some of the things that may be going on in your lives.

This is something we all do and don't even give it another thought. Think about the times that you were struggling with believing in God for some area in your life, and you just over looked things and let it go. You didn't address it, you just went on and made the decision on your own, or you just told that person you were having a problem with to get lost. It seemed like God wasn't going to answer so you did it your way. The Bible calls that sin.

Unfortunately, it took most of us a very long time to be able to come to this conclusion. The trouble comes in when you are saved, and no one takes the time to explain these things to you, and to give you examples from their lives, where God met them and taught them about His faithfulness. We have all of these examples in the Bible of God in the lives of those there, coupled with how He has dealt with you can encourage the new believer and help them to walk.

Where do we find all of these things? In the Bible! "Faith comes from what is heard, and what is heard comes through the message about Christ." Some would say that we have Bible studies in church, they could come to them and learn, and that is part of it, but it takes someone that befriends them, and comes along side of them, and opens their lives to the new believer, and invest their lives into the new believer. When this happens the new believer begins to grow by leaps and bounds.

It takes someone that wants to take the Word of God at face value, and wants to see new Christians begin to mature in their walk. It takes someone who isn't afraid of getting their hands dirty, and someone who is willing to face the struggles they are facing with them, someone who exhibits the love of Jesus Christ to them, someone who remembers where they came from and the struggles that they faced when they were babies in Christ.

This is not an easy task. Sometimes the things that the person faces is really hard, and you may feel that you don't have any answers for them, and in yourself you don't, but God always has the right Word for them in His Word. Sometimes you feel that you don't know the Word of God well enough to be able to do this. Listen to what is being said by that statement. There is no time like the present to get to know God's Word, not just for you, but so you can give it away to someone else and comfort him or her.

This is the ministry that God has called all of us to. This is part of the Great Commission. This isn't just for the pastor, or the evangelist, this is for everyone, and it takes everyone to be involved to bring people up in the Lord. We have to stop just giving birth, and we must start becoming mentors, and friends, brothers and sisters, and we must love them enough to lead them into an intimate relationship with Jesus.

The Mind:

Most of us, who have been Christian for a long time, have heard things about being a new creation in Christ, and have heard that the old has past away, and all things are new. And we believe this, for the most part, because some things in our lives did go away, but other things remained, and it is those things that have remained we are baffled about.

Second Corinthians chapter 10:3-6 talks about this problem that we all face, and it is something that we need to look at. "For although we are walking in the flesh, we do not rage war in a fleshly way, since the weapons of our warfare are not fleshly, but are powerful through God for the demolition of strongholds. We demolish arguments and every high-minded thing that is raised up against the knowledge of God, taking every thought captive to the obedience of Christ. And we are ready to punish any disobedience, once your obedience is complete."

It is very important to look at, and to listen to the words that are spoken in this passage. Through this passage we can gain great insight into the understanding of how we do overcome as Christians in our daily battle to live the Christian life according to God's plan. We too often think that God has done it all and we don't have a part in it. It is true that God has given us all we need to live this life. 2 Peter 1:3 says, "For His divine power has given us everything required for life and godliness, through the knowledge of Him who called us by His own glory and goodness."

Scripture says that we have all that we need, so why am I fighting constantly in my life to live the Christian life? The key lies in 2 Cor. 10:3-6. It starts off by telling us that we walk in the flesh, and this reference is not that we walk according to the flesh, but that we are alive and living in this world. This means that because we are living in this world there are things that are going to oppose the Christian way of life.

The good news is that Paul says that even though we are living on this earth, and that evil surrounds us, we do not fight against it the way people in the flesh do. We are in the middle of war in Iraq. How are we fighting the battle? With guns and airplanes, and bombs. We, as Christians, do not fight the evil in this world that way. The Bible says that our weapons, and yes we do have weapons, are not like those of this world. Ours are powerful through God. Some versions say, they are divinely powerful, which I like because to be divinely means that it comes from God. Our weapons that we use for battle against the flesh are from God.

The natures of these weapons are for the destruction of strongholds. A strong hold is a fortified place, a place that has been built so that it is difficult for anything, or anyone to come in and tear it down. We all have seen these kinds of places as we have watched movies, they are called castles. When we see these castle, they are not only places that are very big, but they are made of stones with very thick walls and draw bridges, with moots around them, these are places that are built to keep unwanted people out, and those that are inside safe.

Now how does that relate to us? Let's go deeper. The Scripture in 2 Cor. 10:4-5 says that, these strongholds are arguments, and high-minded ideas that are against the knowledge of God. We over the years, before we were Christians were taught things, and we thought we learned things that seemed right to us. These are things that we have used to protect ourselves from hurt, or we have heard things about God that seemed right, and it came from people that we trusted.

Strongholds are things that we think that are not correct about life and God, or maybe practices, which come from thoughts, that do not line up with God's Word. Have you ever heard the old story of the mother who was getting a holiday ham ready for cooking? As she was getting this ham ready, her daughter was watching her. The mother took the ham, before she put it in the roaster, and cut both ends off of the ham, then she put it in the roaster. The little girl then asked her mother why she cut those ends off?

The mother's response was that, that is the way she learned from her mother. The mother had thought that that was the way you cooked the ham. Becoming curious the mother went back to her mother, who went back to her mother. Too make a long story short, it had nothing to do with how to cook a ham, it had to do with the great-great grandmother had a roaster that the ham wouldn't fit, so she cut the ends off of the ham so it would fit. We do the same things in our lives; the trouble is that our thoughts don't line up with God's Word.

What we have to do is this, we must take our thoughts about God and the way we think we are suppose to live, measure them against God's Word, and everything that doesn't line up with God's Word, we are to change our minds about what we have been believing, and change our thoughts to what God says is right. As this happens the strongholds in our lives are torn down, and our lives begin to change, because our minds have changed.

Think about this for a minute, even common sense would tell us that we really don't know too much about God when we first come to the Lord and are saved. We start learning more as we are taught by our pastors, and Sunday School Teachers. The trouble is that we still have false ideas about God long after we have been Christians for awhile. If that isn't true then way do we have such a hard time believing that God will intervene in our situations?

The reason for this is that we still are not thinking about God correctly. Or what about the times that we think that God isn't listening to us as we pray, or that He didn't hear us about a certain prayer that we prayed? Or even worse that He didn't answer a prayer that we prayed.

The Word of God says that He hears our prayers, and that He answers our prayers, so if I am thinking that He didn't hear or answer, then I have a strong hold in my mind, and I am not thinking about God correctly. I must go back to the Word of God and chose to believe what His Word says about Him and my situation.

Sometimes we don't think that we have strong holds in our lives anymore until we look at it like this. This is important for us to see, because if we have those strong holds, and we have been Christians for some time, then think about those people that have jus come to know the Lord.

If we would recognize our own situation, then we would be more patient with the new born babes that have just come to the Lord. And we would be able to help them understand what this passage is talking about. And this would help them see the things in their lives that are not lining up with God's Word.

If we could get a handle on this we would see great victories in our lives and the churches lives as well. Think about it for a minute, if everyone was able to see the areas in their lives that didn't measure up to the truth and was able to turn to God's Word, their lives would be spent in victory as the Word of God says that we are.

We are in need of being able to listen to others as well. What I mean by this is that when people come to us and point out these areas in our lives we need to be able to humble ourselves and listen to them. It is hard to have someone else, especially if they are younger in the Lord than you, come to you and point out an area in your life that doesn't measure up to God's Word.

Know I am talking about taking it to heart instead of just smiling and saying thank- you, and walking away thinking they really need to grow up before they tell you what needs to be done. There is another strong hold in our minds, thinking I know more than they do. Remember, Scripture says that knowledge puffs up. Pride is certainly at work when we think that we know too much to be concerned about the correction of someone we think is less mature than us.

Our minds and the things that we have learned over the years are very strong, or to say it better or to be more blunt, our pride is too large to think that we don't always think correctly. If we are still sinning then we are not thinking correctly. We need to show new people that we are willing to live the Christian life, and we desire our strong holds to be torn down by God's Word as well.

Think about the witness we would be for the new ones in our midst if we were to recognize openly our own short comings, and confess and repent of them. We could teach them how to turn to God's Word and apply it to our lives. We could show them how Christian spiritual warfare is really fought, and how the Christian continues in the victory that Christ promised us. That is really being the church that we are supposed to be with each other and those in a lost world.

CHAPTER 2

Life Application

Sometimes, in the church today, we think that when we come to be Christians that all we have to do, is repent, and read the Word of God and believe. If we do these things then something mysterious will happen and we will be changed, and our whole life will be the life of Christ.

In theory this is good, but in the Bible this is not the case for any of us. We have a responsibility to begin to practice the things that God outlines for us in the Bible. There is a life application that we are responsible for, and as this happens, God, will empower us to live the Christian life He has called us to.

The Bible exhorts people about their practices. We as people are either going to practice that which is not good, or we are going to practice that which is good. Listen to Proverbs 23:12, "Apply yourself to instruction and listen to words of knowledge." This passage is telling us that whatever instruction we have received, we need to apply to our lives.

Apply means to put to use. This means that what we receive as instruction from the Word of God needs to be put to use in our lives. If we don't put it to use it is useless to us. It is just empty words that we can hear any where to us. Instruction, for it to be useful for us must be put to use, or it will not affect our lives in the least since.

Being a Christian is not the wimpy life that some would have you believe. Being a Christian takes great strength and character to live out. Many people hear the Word of God, but not all apply the Word of God, or put to use the Word of God to their lives. Proverbs is full of instruction, that for us to receive we must put to use in our lives.

An example of this is in the same chapter of Proverbs in verse 19, it says, "Listen, my son, and be wise; Keep your mind on the right course." We all know that if we are headed to a place in our lives losing focus of the goal will affect the outcome of our plans, it will get us side tracked. So this verse would be a good one to put to use in our lives. It tells us to keep our minds on the goals that we have set for ourselves.

In this case it speaks of setting our goals to be that of God's instruction, and not letting ourselves get side track to where we loose focus of the path we are on, and the destination to where we are headed. I had a track coach that told me to never look at the runners that were behind you, to keep my eye on the finish line. He said that if I looked around behind me that I would not only loose focus, but also I would loose stride as well. He was right!

So we find that this passage of Scripture, when put to use in our lives can, and will help keep us on course. We will not get side tracked and loose focus of the goal for our lives. And this gives a good example of what it means to put the Scripture, or the instruction of God to use in our lives.

So Scripture is not only to be heard, or listened to and read, but it is to be but to use in our lives as well. If we do not do this it is to stay in the same place as we are now and not grow in the Lord. It is too stay a baby Christian, only able to receive the milk of the Word and not the meat.

It comes down to a decision for us. Do we want to grow in the Lord? Or do we want to stay and do nothing? Let me give you a caution here. To stay and do nothing is not to stay in the same place and be static, but instead it will lead us into decline in our lives and right back to the same things that we left, that we didn't want in our lives.

Bad Examples:

Fortunately, the Bible isn't just a book that tells us all of the things that we are supposed to do, and then just leave it at that. The Bible also tells and gives us bad examples of people that do not apply God's Word to their lives, or who apply it in a wrong way.

Too many times, we as church people tell others what they should be doing, and we do things another way. We have all heard this from our parents who say, "Do as I say, not as I do". And in some of the cases that I have been aware of that is pretty good advise. The trouble is that I did do as they did, and it got me in trouble when I did.

That is the trouble that I am talking about. People are not going to do what you tell them as much as they are going to do what you do, especially if they look up to you. Pay attention pastor's this is for you. People that come to your church and hear you speak think that you are above all the stuff that they go through. They will not admit it but they do think like that.

The trouble is that when they see you living differently than what you preach, it pretty much shakes their faith to the core. This is spoken of in a couple of different places in the Scriptures. In Matt. 23:2-3 it says, "The scribes and the Pharisee's are seated in the chair of Moses. Therefore do whatever they tell you and observe it. But don't do what they do, because they don't practice what they teach."

To sit in the chair of Moses is to be the teacher of the people. This is a place that people came to in the synagogue to be taught from the Scriptures in how to live their lives according to the Word of God. And they came to hear this from leaders who were suppose to know what the Word of God said, and be putting into practice those things that they told others to do.

Unfortunately, these teachers that were teaching the people from the Word of God were not putting into practice it their own lives. So Jesus tells the people to do what they are taught, but not to follow the lives of these teachers, because they were living a lie.

This goes for all of us. It isn't just the pastor that needs to take heed about this; it is all of the people that are teaching others. This lesson is for Sunday Schools Teachers, Deacons, and Elders, everyone that others look up to as a mature Christian. We are to be teaching them God's Word, and showing them how to put these lessons into practice by living it out in our lives.

This is teaching people Life Application. Anything short of this is the same thing that Jesus had to say about the scribes and the Pharisee's. The question to ask ourselves is this, if Jesus came to our church, and observed me as I was teaching the people, what would He tell the people about my teaching? Would He tell them to not only follow the teaching that I am giving, but would He also tell them to follow my example as well?

Paul talks about this same thing. He is talking to the church about eating meat that has been sacrificed to idols. Paul tells the church that he understands that it is okay for some of them to eat meat that has been sacrificed to idols. Some there realized that there is only one God, and this meat was neither, good or bad in itself, but there was another principle that needed to be followed here.

The principle that needs to be followed is one that is based in love. Some of the people that were in the church at that time were converts from the pagan religions that did this sacrifice of the meat to the idols. That is what they were saved from. Their understanding was that the meat was sacrificed to demons, evil gods, gods that they had been saved from. They wanted nothing more than to be free from that. Yet there were those in the church that had been going to the pagan temple market, and buying this meat and eating it in their homes.

The church had taught them that the pagan temple practices were evil and ought to be discontinued because they were displeasing to God, and then they go and buy this meat that had been sacrificed to these gods. What kind of statement is that? It would be the same thing if someone came to church and got saved and was an alcoholic. We would tell them that they needed to stay away from alcohol. Now what if that person, who accepted what we said, saw us going into the store and buying a bottle of wine? What would you say to them about that, and how could you explain that to them? Paul says that we ought not cause someone to stumble so that we can practice our freedom.

The whole point is this, if we are going to teach our people, especially those that are new Christians, about what it means to be a Christian, and teach them about applying the Word of God to our lives, then we ought to be applying it to our lives. When they look at us they ought to be able to see what it looks like when the Word of God is lived out. We ought to be good examples and not bad ones.

Managers and Servants

I remember when I was a kid that I had heroes that I would look up to. Back then we had Superman on T.V. and I would watch that without fail. Batman was another Super hero that I thought highly of. He would swing down on criminals from high buildings and fight and always win against evil.

I would try to be like these guys, because I looked up to them. I remember that we had a fence all the way around the yard. The fence was no ordinary fence, because it was high, to me then it was, maybe six feet high. I would put a cape on, climb to the top of that fence and jump off trying to fly, pretending that I was Superman going after the bad guy.

I would also wear a mask over my face and pretend that I was Batman going after the bad guy, working hard at saving my city from evil. These were figures that I looked up to when I was very young. And does anyone remember the Green Hornet? But there came a time that I went for the more realistic heroes. The Lone Ranger was one of those heroes.

As I got older my heroes changed from fictional figures to real life heroes, like police officers, or fireman, people that really saved people from harm's way. These guys never seemed to be concerned about their own safety, they were always more concerned over the wellbeing of those they were trying to save.

I remember that I knew this guy that was older than I was, and He joined the army and became a soldier. He was someone that I really looked up to. These were the people that I thought were my heroes. Kids always need heroes, people to look up to, people that they could try and walk in their footsteps.

The truth of the matter is that we all have people that we look up to. Today, people have less of those heroes that can be seen. The trouble is that many people today are looking at the bad guys as their heroes. Look around us at the sports figures that people are looking up to. These are guys that are doing drugs, and getting into trouble with the law.

The heroes that we looked up to were people that did good, and they lived a good life. The life that they lived measured up to the life that they were telling others to live. They were heroes because they were people that lived what they preached; they exhibited a moral, good life to the people that they were dealing with. When they got a bad guy, they didn't have to worry about something they had done catching up to them. Their lives were an example of clean living.

The writer of Hebrews had this same thing in mind when he wrote in Heb. 6:11-12, "Now we want each of you to demonstrate the same diligence for the final realization of your hope, so that you won't become lazy, but imitators of those who inherit the promises through faith and perseverance."

The writer is telling us what we are to put to practice, in our lives, the things that we have seen those that have gone before us put to practice. As the heroes of the faith that have gone before us put to practice in their lives the things of those that were before them, we are to put into practice in our lives the things that they did. And we are to be examples through that to those that are coming into the church now.

Those that are being saved now need heroes of the faith. They need you to live out your faith in their lives in a way that they can see it and apply it to their lives. They need to have people that are willing to be open with them, people that will share their shortcomings as well as their strengths. They need people that are willing to invest in their lives, and dare to get close.

These people are the ones that the Bible calls servants and managers. There is a song that says that you want to be great in God's Kingdom, then you must be a servant of all. And really that is what being a servant is really about. It is sharing your life with others, giving of yourself. That is exactly what the heroes that I remember did, they shared their lives with others, so they could save them from peril.

This, by the way, is also the definition of love. 1 John 3:16, "This is how we have come to know love: He laid down His life for us. We should also lay our down our lives for our brothers." Jesus is that hero by every definition of the word. He came and defeated evil for us by putting His life on the line for us. And we are to do the same for one another.

Think about this for a minute. Jesus came to our defense when there were no others to do that for us. He came to our defense when we didn't even deserve it. In the stories that we watched as kids about heroes, they came to save the victims. We were guilty, not victims, and yet He came to save us anyway.

We are called to follow in the footsteps of Jesus. We are called to lay our lives down for our brothers. This comes in the form of being there to someone that is just starting out in this new Christian life. We are to come along side of them, and teach them to live the Christian life by sharing our life with them.

Love:

You may be saying, what does love have to do with life application? It has everything to do with life application of Scripture. The truth of the matter is, that we cannot be a good manager, or servant without loving those that we have been called to manage, or to serve.

We must, as said before, follow in the footsteps of Jesus. This is what is said about Jesus and love. 1 John 3:16-20, "This is how we have come to know love: He laid His life down for us. We should also lay down our lives for our brothers. If anyone has this world's goods and sees his brother in need but shuts off his compassion from him-how can God's love reside in him?

Little children, we must not love in word or speech, but in deed and truth; that is how we will know we are of truth, and will convince our hearts of His presence, because if our hearts condemn us, God is greater than our hearts and knows all things."

What this is saying is this, Jesus is our supreme example of love, and He showed us His love for us when He allowed Himself to be nailed to the cross for us, He laid His life down for us. And John goes on to say that because He did, we are to also lay our lives down for our brothers. To lay our lives down means that we are there for our brothers and sisters when they need us. We make sure that our brothers and sisters have their needs met, through the abundance that God has given us. If we have what our brothers and sisters need, we are to make sure that they have it. John goes on to say that anything less than that is just empty words.

John says that we are to openly show our compassion for those that God has put into our lives through the church. And we openly show, or the fruit of compassion is seen through our action, love is a verb, it is an action word. Love is not just a descriptive word, but love takes action.

The meaning of compassion is that we are conscience of another's need and we are seeking to alleviate their suffering. How many times are we aware of our brothers and sisters needs, and we tell them that we will pray for them, and just walk away without doing anything about it? We see their needs, but we have no intention of trying to alleviate it. That is loving with words only and according to this passage is not true love at all.

How wonderful it is to have servants and managers that put to practice the things that Scripture tells us. How wonderful it is to see churches that love people, and we are able to see that love through the actions that they take on behalf of those in the body that are hurting and suffering.

Stop right here and just think with me for a moment. Think about what the church would look like if we were doing ministry that way. Jesus said that the world would know who we were by our love for one another. Think what the world would be saying and thinking about the church if they were to see this in action. In this world it is pretty hard to deny true love in action. They would be seeing Jesus in the church. He would be the head of the church, and people would be drawn to that kind of love.

Think of the church in worship if that kind of love were to reign in the church. With that kind of love in the church worship service would be filled with the presence of the Holy Spirit, and we would see things done by the Lord that we can only imagine right now. If that kind of love reigned in the church there would be no broken relationships, or divisions, we would be of one mind, that of Christ.

The church would also be taking charge of the things that we have given over to the government to handle. These are things that the church, at one time in history, handled themselves. The churches would never have a financial problem because people would be tithing, and those that were coming into the church would be taught to tithe. The church would have all the money and resources that they need to carryout the Lord's business.

People would be hungry to hear what you have to say, because they would see this huge difference in you that they did not see in themselves. They would be hungry fore that change to take place in them. And all of this by just doing the things that Scripture says that we are to be doing. And then teaching others to apply these same principles to their lives. What a wonderful thought!

CHAPTER 3

Ministry

We discussed in chapter 1 the way we minister, but I would like to go into more depth here if we can. Paul was talking to the church in Corinth about ministry, and specifically how to do ministry. If there is any question that I get from Christians it has to do with how to minister.

Three questions come to mind that are the most asked questions: What are my gifts? How do I find out what they are? And, how do I minister to people? Paul seems to answer them all here in this passage.

The first thing is that He, meaning God, comforts us. This is important for us to know. It is through Him that we are able to know all that we need to know. If we look at Jesus, scripture says, then we have seen the Father. This is important, because if we look at Jesus we can see how He ministered to us. The reason that this is important is that it will be the same way that we minister to others.

How did Jesus come to you and minister to you? What is the one thing that you can say about Jesus and the way that He came to you? As for me, He knew every intimate detail of my life. He knew all of the ugliness of my life. He knew even the things that I was not willing to look at myself.

The Samaritan at the well experienced Him the same way in John 4:4-25. Jesus told His disciples to go on ahead of Him and get some food to eat, meanwhile Jesus went to a place called Jacob's well. While He was there a Samaritan women came to draw water from the well. When she got there, Jesus asked her for a drink of water. Understand that this woman was at the well at a time that no other women would be there. That was because of her life style, she couldn't be around the well when the others were there. She was a social outcast, someone to be looked down on.

The next thing to look at was that she was a Samaritan woman which is someone that the Jews would have never been around. They were looked down on by the Jews, and they would have been completely ignored by the Jews, much less talked to, and even more surprising they would have never asked her for a drink of water.

Jesus also knew about her life style. He knew that she had, had five husbands previous to the man that she was living with. She wasn't even married to this man she was living with. She was living in sin, and she was not feeling all good about it. You can tell that by the way she phrased her statement to Jesus. When Jesus told her to go and get her husband she just told that Him I don't have a husband. She didn't say anything beyond that.

When I was living in the world, and I was around people that would look down on my life style I didn't give them anymore information than was needed, and suppose if you think about it and are truthful with yourselves, you were much like that as well. My excuse was that my life is none of their business.

We can see Jesus at work here in this encounter. Jesus wasn't put out by the fact that she was a woman, which is not the way others would have been around her. When Jesus looked at her he saw someone that needed His love, and salvation. He also wasn't conscience of her race, love never sees what color or what their differences are, and their only concern is how to extend the love of the Lord to them.

Jesus wasn't shocked by her life style. He knew all about her divorces, and her living with this other man. Even though He addressed it, He didn't make a big issue of it. Sin needs to be addressed, but it doesn't need to be harped on. She knew that He knew of her life style, and she also saw that He wasn't put off by her. He still had a Godly concern for her. He knew that she needed what He was offering. He also knew that she was hungry for Him and what He was offering. Many of the people we run into that have these life styles that are completely foreign to us, now that we are Christians, are just looking for love and acceptance, although in the wrong way.

The truth of the matter is that many of us, before we became Christians, lived life style that were similar and that is what we were looking for. Jesus knew what she was looking for, and He offered her the true way to live and find that love and acceptance that she was looking for.

Jesus knows our hearts, and He knows the way we are, and the things that we go through. Jesus deals with us from an intimate knowledge of what we are going through. The reason that He is able to do that is that He went through what we go through. He just didn't sin and give into it like we have.

It says in Hebrews 4:14-16, "Therefore since we have a great high priest who has passed through the heavens-Jesus the Son of God-let us hold fast to the confession. For we do not have a high priest who is unable to sympathize with our weaknesses, but One who has been tested in every way as we are, yet without sin. Therefore let us approach the throne of grace with boldness, so that we may receive mercy and find grace to help us at the proper time."

When Jesus walked the earth, He was tempted in everyway that I have been tempted. This is comforting because He is someone that knows what I am going through. He is someone who can understand my weaknesses, and fears. He is someone that understands my need for love and acceptance. So He is one that I can turn to when I am going through the troubles and temptations of this life.

That is what is meant when 2 Corinthians chapter one says that He is the God of all comfort, and we are to comfort others the same way that He comforted us. We are to know the weaknesses of those that come into our paths, because of the intimate knowledge we have of our own weaknesses. And we are to sympathize with them, and comfort them in the love, mercy and grace that God did for us.

That means that we are to look beyond all of the races, social outcasts, and sins and see them as those that God loves, and because God loves them we are to love them too. We have, because of Jesus, the very thing they are looking for, and we need to offer to them that love and acceptance, as freely as God offered it to us. We need to follow the example given to us in Scripture by God as He ministered to others.

Spiritual Gifts

This is an area that many people are confused about. Some today deny the existence of spiritual gifts, or at least a portion of them. Still others are longing to know what their spiritual giftedness is. And there are still others that think that if they use their gifts in the church that is all that is needed, they are fulfilling their purpose in this life that God has given to us all.

Nothing could be farther from the truth. Spiritual gifts are just an aspect of service to our Lord, and to one another. Our lives are to be lived in submission to the Lord, and we have to fulfill His purpose for our lives, which goes beyond just church service. The reason that we are saved is to touch others for Christ. That is why we are filled with the Holy Spirit.

But first I would like to discuss whether or not spiritual gifts are for today. It is baffling to me that we can say that we believe the Word of God to be inerrant, or without error, and at the same time say that there are things in the Bible, especially the New Testament that are not for us today.

The writers of the New Testament wrote these letters to the churches of that day, yet the Holy Spirit uses these writings to speak to us today about God, our relationship with one another, and the things that ought to be happening in the church. Hebrews 13:8 says, "Jesus Christ is the same yesterday, today, and forever."

If Jesus Christ is the same yesterday, today and forever, how could he change in the way that He deals with us today, and the way that He dealt with the church yesterday? And more important, where does it tell us in the Bible that He took any of these things away? And who has the authority to make changes for God?

The Bible doesn't say that any of the gifts were removed or changed. In fact, the Bible says that these things ought to be done by those that are believers. In Mark 16:17-18 it says, "And these signs will accompany those who believe: In My name they will drive out demons; they will speak with new tongues; they will pick up snakes; if they should drink anything deadly, it will never harm them; they will lay hands on the sick and they will get well."

If we are believers, the Bible says that these things ought to be happening. I would think that when the Bible says these things that people who calm to be Christians would want to fit into the pattern that Scripture has laid out for believers. Unfortunately, today many Christians are divided over what the Bible says is true. They, for some reason, do not feel that these things are for us today, which says what they really feel about the Bible being inerrant.

I would ask these individuals this question, if that is wrong what other parts of the Bible are wrong as well? And, who gave them the authority to change what the Bible says about such things? For those that are teaching such things, they might consider that they will have some explaining to do before God one day. If the Bible says it we ought to believe it, that is my philosophy.

I would like to clear up one more thing before we go on. All of us are called to witness for the Lord to the lost. I have heard some say that they are not gifted to share the gospel that they are gifted in a specific area and they go on to let me know what area that is in. The Bible calls us all to the Great Commission. We are all called to share the good news with the lost.

The Holy Spirit indwelt us for a couple of reasons; one of those reasons is to share Jesus Christ with those that don't know Him. Listen to what is said in Matt. 28:18-20, "Then Jesus came near and said to them, All authority has been given to Me in heaven and on earth. Go, therefore, and make disciples of all nations, baptizing them in the name of the Father and of the Son and of the Holy Spirit, teaching them to observe everything I have commanded you. And remember, I am with you always, to the end of the age."

Some may say that it was the 11 that Jesus told to go, and they would be right, but He told the 11 to teach the disciples that they make to follow all that He had commanded them, and that is to go. We are all called to go and preach the gospel to the world, baptizing them in the name of the Father and the Son and the Holy Spirit. Witnessing is to be in conjunction with the gifts. We cannot do one without doing the other and still be obedient Disciples of Christ.

So, some may ask what are the gifts of the Spirit and how are they to be used? It really is a three fold answer. First, the gifts are the Holy Spirit at work through the saints. He is showing Himself through the saints. When the saints are working in the gifts of the Spirit it is really the Holy Spirit being seen through them. In 1 Cor. 12:7 it says, "A manifestation of the Spirit is given to each person to produce what is beneficial." Manifestation of the Spirit is the Spirit showing Himself through a particular person.

Also in chapter 12 of 1 Cor. we find a list of the gifts that are given. I want you to understand that these are not an exhaustive list of the gifts. There are sub categories under these descriptions. We are able to see many more gifts that are obviously the Holy Spirit in churches that are operating in the gifts. And in the second half of the same chapter is gifts that are leadership gifts, and we will discuss that later.

Second, the gifts are for the building up of the body. Each of us has a gift from the Holy Spirit, and we are to use those gifts to build each other up, and we ought to have concern for one another. That is what is said in the whole of chapter 12. So the gifts are for the body or the church.

The gifts are also for the lost. In Acts chapter 4 the Apostles were arrested for preaching the gospel of Christ, and they were told not to ever do that again. They walked away from there after telling them they were going to follow what God told them to do. They went back to the church, told the church what they were told, and they began to pray. In their prayer they prayed for boldness to continue to preach the gospel, but they also prayed that the Lord would confirm the gospel spoken with signs and wonders. Listen to verses 29-30 of chapter 4, "And now, Lord, consider their threats, and grant that Your slaves may speak with complete boldness, while you stretch out your hand for healing, signs, and wonders to be performed through the name of Your holy Servant Jesus."

So here they are, praying that there be confirmation of the Word that is to be preached to the lost, and they would know that it is the truth through signs and wonders, and people getting healed. Didn't Jesus Himself heal those that came to Him, and weren't some of the things said about Him because of the signs and wonders that He did stating that He had to be the Son of God. Even the day that He was crucified and the skies turned dark and the storm came served to the guards to help them understand that He had to have been the Son of God.

Next there are gifts that are leadership gifts. In Eph. chapter 4, Paul speaks of leadership gifts, and identifies them as apostles, prophets, evangelists, pastors and teachers. The purpose of these gifts is for teaching and equipping the saints. This passage says that these are so that the body would mature in the stature of Christ. Growing up to be like Christ, and so that the church will not be thrown about by every wind of doctrine that comes along. And also the word apostle here is in lower case, many others other than the Apostles. It would lead one to believe that there still ought to be an office of apostle in the church.

These things are all for ministry and must be understood. But not only should they be understood, but they ought to be accepted and applied to our lives. The Lord called us to unity in Him. And He tells us to agree with one another. That means that we are to go to the Bible and learn to agree on what He says in the Bible. It is not good enough to agree to disagree, the Bible says that we are to agree with one another. We are to take what He says in His Word to heart, and quite finding things in it to divide over. We are to be at work in His service showing our love for one another to a lost world.

An Example from Moses

Sometimes we make ministry more difficult than it needs to be. The truth is that sometimes we try and do it all by ourselves. This comes from lack of knowledge, and sometimes from lack of trust in others. Even though we just talked about the Spiritual gifts being given to all Christians, and that they are for the building up of the body, we don't trust others to be able to do the job, or we don't know who is able to do the job.

If the body is to truly be built up, then it needs all of the body performing all the jobs that Christ has given the body to do. Unfortunately, when this doesn't happens there are hard feelings that takes place, and those that are trying to do it all suffer burnout and most often quit doing the job themselves, leaving no one doing anything.

Pastors do this all of the time. Some feel that there is no one able to do the job the way that they can, after all they were "trained" to do ministry. This is a wrong understanding of God's Word for them to take that position, and they need to go back and take a hard look at what God's Word says about the body and body life. They don't understand as they ought to.

Sometimes it is about wanting to look good to people. Someone will take over doing all of the things in the church, after all no one will step up to the plate, or they just don't do the job like I can. They take over this large amount of work, and when people don't recognize them and their efforts, they get mad and quit. And they go through all of these things telling people how much they have done, and if they were to leave the church it would fall apart.

Jethro, Moses father-in-law noticed Moses doing everything one day when he was visiting Moses, and he pointed out some things that would help Moses organize better and be able to have ministry done in such a way that other people's gifts were used, and Moses wouldn't suffer burnout.

We find this wise advice in Exodus 18:13-23, "The next day Moses sat down to judge the people, and they stood around Moses from morning until evening. When Moses' father-in-law saw everything he was doing for them he asked, What is this thing you're doing for the people? Why are you alone sitting as judge, while all the people stand around you from morning until evening? Moses replied to his father-in-law, Because the people come to me to inquire of God. Whenever they have a dispute, it comes to me, and I make a decision between one man and another. I teach them God's statutes and laws. What you are doing is not good, Moses father-in-law said to him. You will certainly wear out both yourself and these people who are with you, because the task is too heavy for you. You can't do it alone. Now listen to me; I will give you some advice, and God be with you. You be the one to represent the people before God and bring their cases to Him. Instruct them about the statutes and laws, and teach them the way to live and what they must do. But you should select from all the people able men, God-fearing, trustworthy, and hating bribes. Place them over people as officials of thousands, hundreds, fifties, and tens. They should judge the people at all times. Then they can bring you every important case but judge every minor case themselves. In this way you will lighten your load, and they will bear it with you. If you do this, and God so directs you, you will be able to endure, and also all these people will be able to go home satisfied."

Here is Moses taking on all of the responsibility himself. He is the only one that can do these things. He is the only one that can teach these people what God is saying to them. Understand, Moses is responsible for teaching the people, he is the pastor, he is to equip the saints, but if he doesn't equip them so they can do ministry, he is doing a injustice to them and they will not be carrying out their God given responsibilities.

But here early in the life of Israel, we start to hear about burnout and what causes burnout. Burnout comes when we take on responsibilities that are not ours to take on. And Jethro explained this to Moses. But I want you to see that it will burnout our people when we are taking on the entire job and not empowering them to do what God called them to do.

It is the pastor's responsibility to teach the people, or the church, to do the job, and what God says about the way we are to live, but we are to find the people that God has called to do these things in the church, and we are to give them those jobs, and empower them to do the job. And when they have trouble, then they can come to us, and we can guide them what ought to be done. In this way the pastor is not dealing with everyone, but with only a few. Jesus did this same thing with His disciples. He dealt with twelve men, and they dealt with the others.

One other thing must be said here. Do not micro manage them after you have given them the job. When you are looking over their shoulder, giving them "Direction" you will chase them away, and it will create hard feelings, and they will know that you don't trust them. They will fail from time to time, but help them up, dust them off, and teach them anything they may need to know about the problem they encountered, and let them go at it again.

When the church is run like it is suppose to be run, the church can grow, and people will be excited about what is happening in their lives and in the lives of those in the church. They will also become apart of what is going on in the church.

CHAPTER 4

Qualifications for Ministry

It is interesting to me how the Bible could say that when we come to Christ we are new creations in Him, and that all things are new, there is now no slave, man, women, Greek, and so forth, and still we hold things against those that come and not let them serve in the church. We tell them because their past was the way it was they are not able to serve, and then they use the Bible to try and prove their point.

The problem that they are going to run into is the grace of God, through Jesus Christ, and them forcing an interpretation on Scripture that Scripture will not support. The Bible tells us that we need to divide the Word of God correctly. Forcing interpretations on Scripture is not dividing Scripture correctly. Not to mention they are serving to discourage people from the new life that the Bible had promised them.

It is equally interesting to me, that when people fall into sin even after being a Christian, the church, many times doesn't allow those to serve. If Christ can forgive them, then why can't we forgive them as well. To hold sin against people is a form of unforgiveness.

The Bible calls us to restore a brother or sister when they have fallen. The Bible does speak to those that refuse to repent, but if a brother or sister repents, then why is it that we don't forgive them, and restore them. But instead many times we not only don't restore them, but we talk about them, point fingers at them, and in some case act like they have some disease that is contagious.

The Bible tells us, in Matt. 26:69-75, that Peter had denied the Lord Jesus. And not only did he deny Jesus, but he denied Jesus after being warned that he was going to do so. All of us have been in a position that when someone came and accursed us of something we were so afraid of the out come that we struggled and, at least, had thought about lying to protect our selves, in fact most of us have lied to protect our selves at one point in our lives or another.

Peter, being afraid, when he was identified as having been a disciple of Christ, and was watching on as they had beaten Jesus and were about to crucify Him, knowing that if he told them the truth that would be his fate too, lied to protect himself. Peter had sinned, and he had sinned against the one that had loved him dearly. Peter knew that he had committed a grievous against Jesus his Lord. He knew that so much that Scripture tells us that he wept bitterly and took off to go back fishing. In Peter's mind everything was over for him. Ministry was out of the question, he was a coward, and had betrayed the one that he had claimed love for.

Remember, Peter's comment to the Lord in the upper room was that he had a sword, and he would defend the Lord with his sword. And he did when he was in the garden surrounded by his friends, thinking they could win this battle. But now the Lord was going to die, there was no hope of victory in a fight, and he was alone to make a stand by himself, and he had failed to make that stand, instead he had been a coward and denied even knowing Jesus to protect his own skin.

The writer of Hebrews asked a question that was going through his mind about this same thing. In Hebrews 6:4-6, "For it is impossible to renew to repentance those who were once enlightened, who tasted the heavenly gift, became companions with the Holy Spirit, tasted God's good word and the powers of the coming age, and who have fallen away, because, to their own harm, they are recrucifing the Son of God and holding Him up to contempt."

What the writer is saying is this: If someone has tasted the good things of God, including the Holy Spirit, and then denies all of this to protect themselves how could this one be saved? And that is our attitude sometimes with the people around us. Look at what they did! How can they possibly be restored? What they did was on out right defiance of the Lord! They could never be brought back and restored in any kind of ministry.

This same question came up in Matt. 19:13-26, only this time it was about a rich man who had come to Jesus and asked Jesus how he could be saved and have eternal life. Jesus told him to go and sell all that he had, and give it to the poor. The Bible tells us that the rich man walked away sad because he had much money. Really, the rich man had a love for his money that was the real problem.

Jesus made the comment that it was hard for a rich man to enter the Kingdom of God. The others heard Him say this and asked how anyone could be saved. Jesus' comment was that it was impossible for man, but with God all things are possible. The truth is we need to think the way Christ thinks when it comes to each other. If left to us, some times, we will not go a restore a brother, after all look at what they did.

Well Jesus gave example of this with Peter. Now remember, Peter had denied Christ, and had taken off, thinking that it was over for him. In the minds of those that he had been with for the last three years it must have been over for them too because no one went after him. But Jesus after he had risen, told his disciples to go get Peter and bring him to the upper room with you. We find this in Mark 16:7, Jesus restores Peter to ministry, in fact, we find Peter taking a leadership role in the upper room, and with the sermon preached that three thousand people got saved.

With man it is impossible, but with God all things are possible. We, as the church, must start thinking, and seeing people the way God sees them. When we do this we find that all things are possible through Christ Jesus who strengthens me. We also need to have the heart of Christ as well. He was the one at the well with a women who was a Samaritan, and who had been divorced, and was commenting fornication, and He offered her living water that would cause her to never thirst again.

Think about it for a minute. How many of us would walk up to a woman at the well, knowing full well what she was like, and offer her salvation? Would we be concerned about who might see us talking to her? Or would we be so ashamed to be seen with someone like that we would just walk away and shake our heads? Remember Jesus didn't. He ministered to her, and He wasn't concerned who saw Him talking to her.

There was a harlot that came in to Him and washed His feet while He was at the house of a Pharisee, and those at that dinner couldn't believe that He would let her touch Him. Jesus was not ashamed, but forgave her of her sins, and used her in ministry. In fact He said that the Scriptures would always tell of her. Where people repent of their sins, Jesus forgives them and restores them. We must follow that same example, where there is repentance, we must forgive and restore.

In fact we are to look at them as new creations; we are to look at them according to the Spirit, according to Paul who says that he looks at no one according to the flesh any longer, but according to the Spirit.

Qualifications for ministry for the Christian

Interesting enough, the qualifications for the Christian to be involved in ministry is that they be saved, asked Jesus to be Lord and Savior of their lives, and be Spirit filled. In fact it is important for people, once they are saved to be serving in some capacity in the church.

The Bible tells us in 1 Cor. 12:30 that all of us have been baptized by one Spirit into one body. And it goes on to tell us that all of us are placed in the body exactly where God wants us to be. In other words, people and their gift are not their own but instead given to them by God.

In fact the gifts are not the people at work, but it is God at work through His church. Verse 7 of chapter 12 tells us this, "A manifestation of the Spirit is given to each person to produce what is beneficial." All the people that come to Christ are indwelt with the Holy Spirit, who manifests Himself through those people in the form of gifts. And the reason for this is for the benefit of the whole body. As we have discussed before, to not allow the Holy Spirit to use you in this capacity is to grieve the Holy Spirit in you. It is also not being obedient to the call of God.

Chapter 12 then goes on to tell us what some of the gifts of the Spirit are. It is important that we see this. The reason it is important is that we are to except people that God has placed into the body, as Him having placed them there. Then we are to expect them to serve in that capacity in the body, regardless of their past lives.

You might raise on objection here and say that is not good because how do we know what they are able to do, and what if they really haven't changed, they are just pretending. When God places them there get to know them that is what we are suppose to do. We are to be a family, and we really can't be a family without getting to know one another. You have a responsibility as leaders to equip them for the work of ministry anyway. What a time to get to know them and to find out what their gifts are, and where God has placed them into the body.

If they are a Spirit filled Christian they are to be serving in the capacity in the church that God has gifted them to do. If we fail to let them serve, then it is us who are grieving the Holy Spirit, and we ought to be the ones that are to be corrected. We need to stop looking at their past and holding their past against them. We are not to disqualify them based on their past. If Jesus has made them a new creation in Him, who are we to keep reminding them of the person that died with Christ at the cross?

That is what we are doing when we hold peoples past against them, but it goes even further than that. If we are not letting people serve that God has placed in the body, then we are crippling the body of Christ. When He places someone that we need in the body in the place He desires, and we say no because of their past, we are casting away part of the body that God placed there to build the rest of the body up.

Think about this for a moment. We are telling God no and saying to Him that these people are not good enough, and we are telling Him that we don't need what they have to contribute, and really saying that we know more than Christ does. Is that really what we want to say to the creator of the universe? I would hope not, in fact I would hope that we are more willing to let Jesus have His way with His body.

It may be us, those of us that are just trying to protect the body that are causing us to have a body that is not as effective as it ought to be, more importantly, as God intended it to be. If you were there when God was putting together a body, would you tell Him that you did not like where the left leg came from so you think that He ought to discard it. If He did that to the body that He created it would start life off walking with a cane and not be able to run the race the way that He intended that person to run.

When we make these decisions for Christ that is exactly what we are saying. And we are making the body a cripple right from the get go. And just as a side note, where did you and I come from? Do we deserve to be in the ministry that we are in? Isn't it only because of the grace of God that we are able to serve

Him? The fact of the matter is that if He had not extended His grace to us we would be lost, headed for hell, and not able to serve Him, because we wouldn't even be part of the body.

Leadership Roles

The Word of God is so good it always has what we need to guide us in every situation we come to. We can find, in the Word of God, what the brand newly formed church used as their guidelines to choose the first deacons of the church. This is really one of the hot buttons for the church today, and it really doesn't have to be.

We can find this passage in Acts 6:1-7. The early church was experiencing growth and numbers were being added to them on a daily basis. Interestingly enough, where there is growth in the church there are also challenges that arise that will try and stop what God is doing, and will try and take our attention off of the things that we know we are to be doing. This is a perfect example of this happening.

There arose a problem in the distribution of the daily rations. The Hellenistic Jewish women were not getting the amount of food that they were supposed to get. So the women complained about the problem to the apostles. You can almost hear this take place if you have ever been involved in a church conflict. They probably said something like this, "I have tried to overlook this problem, but I just can't overlook it anymore. Those Hebrew Jews are getting all of the food, and we Hellenistic Jews are not getting our fair share. We can't even feed our families on what they are giving to us." Have you ever been there?

So after hearing the problem from the Hellenistic Jews that had been going on, the apostles gathered together the entire congregation together, and laid out a plan for them. These apostles had a sense that division was not in the will of God, and they knew that they had to do something to get this problem settled, and they knew that the best way to get things settled is to call the congregation together and involve all of those concerned.

This is where our first deacon came from, so we must pay attention to what they chose as guidelines for picking them. They said choose seven men, of good reputation, and full of the Holy Spirit. Wow! They didn't say choose seven men, present them to us, so that we may do a background check on them, and interview them as to what their past life has been like. They just wanted seven men that were of good reputation.

This phrase "good reputation" in the Greek means that these men were to have a good testimony of Jesus Christ. They were to be good witnesses of the Gospel. They were to be a living testimony as to the saving grace of the risen Jesus Christ who came to save all men from their sins. How many people do we have in leadership that are not witnessing to a lost world? That is our call as Christians to be a testimony of the saving power of our Lord.

This tells us something about the guidelines of leadership roles. They were known by people that were there. They had been a part of the church, and had displayed something that was outstanding among the church, something that made them stand out above the rest. People thought highly of them. People liked them, and most likely liked being around them. But the most outstanding thing was that they needed to be full of the Holy Spirit.

That is an interesting term, to be full of the Holy Spirit. If most people were asked today to point out people who were full of the Holy Spirit could we do it? What does it mean to be full of the Holy Spirit? Some might say, "I know this person, who in every worship service is just in the presence of the Lord. He has tears running down his face, and he is just worshipping for all he is worth. But that is not what they are talking about here.

To be full of the Holy Spirit means to be displaying the fruits of the Spirit in ones life. In Gal. 5:22, we find out that there are certain characteristics that one displays in ones life that give us an indication of whether someone is full of the Holy Spirit or not. They are love, joy, peace, patience, kindness, goodness, faith, gentleness, self-control. When these things are present in someone's life they are full of the Holy Spirit. Remember, this is the Holy Spirit manifesting Himself through this person. This means that this person is submitting to the Holy Spirit. This brings up the next thing, if this person is submitting to the Holy Spirit there ought to be wisdom displayed in what they do.

The reason is this, if they are full of the Holy Spirit, and they are submitting to Him, then they are also submitting to the Word of God. They are living their lives according to the wisdom of God which is found in His Word. They are able to go to Scripture and apply Scripture to their everyday lives. Scripture is their map for life, and they go there to find what God's will is for them and their situation. And they agree with the Word of God, they aren't trying to find their way around what God's Word says to do.

Notice, they weren't judged by their past, but instead they were examined by what was going on in their lives now. I am not saying that if they have done this for one day then they are the ones, but I am saying if this is the pattern in their lives since they have come to Christ, then they are the ones that are qualified to be a deacon. I am also not saying that these people will not struggle with things from time to time. But where they turn to when things get tough is what will indicate where this person is at spiritually.

That's what Paul was saying when he said that he didn't look at people according to the flesh anymore, but according to the spirit. Paul looked for the evidence of the Holy Spirit in someone's life. Do I see the fruits of the Spirit displayed in this person's life? If I don't then they are not what they say they are. This is the same measurement that Paul used when he addressed the Corinthians in chapter 3:1-4, when he told them that they were immature because they were still displaying in their lives the fruits of the flesh, envy, strife.

In Gal. 5:19 Scripture tells us what the fruits of the flesh look like, sexual immorality, moral impurity, promiscuity, idolatry, sorcery, hatred, strife, jealousy, outbursts of anger, selfish ambitions, dissentions, factions, envy, drunkenness, carousing, and anything similar. These are the things that would disqualify an individual from being in leadership, because they tell us that, that person is living in the flesh and is not submitting himself to the Holy Spirit. This person would not display any wisdom, because they are not looking to God's Word for guidance, but are driven by the lusts of their flesh.

Learning to divide the Scripture correctly is key to finding God's man for the church. This is a problem that has existed for a long time. We have walked away from the solid guidelines of Scripture, and have started to choose leaders like the world would find a CEO of a large company. We are not a large company, but instead are the church, the body of the risen Lord.

Divorce

It is interesting to me that people could read the Bible, see what it says and then pick out one thing in it and use it for a tool against others. What I am talking about is the person who is divorced. You could have been a murderer in your past, get saved and still become a pastor, but if you are divorced no one will look at that person, sighting 1 Tim. 3:2. And yet that same verse also says that one has to be above reproach, which means incidentally, that no one is able to bring an acquisition against you. How many of us, and those that are pastors, are able to stand against that? Someone always has an acquisition against pastors, because pastors, by the nature of their job, step on toes.

It also says, in the next two verses that he is not to be quarrelsome, and he is to be self controlled, how many have lost their tempers? All this to say that they pull one thing out of this passage and say he isn't qualified to be a pastor because he has been divorced. Most interestingly is that they have not done a word study, nor have they looked at what Ephesus and Crete were facing at that time in history.

Another thing for us to remember is that all of our modern day versions of the Bible, including, the Kings James versions came from the same original source and that is the Greek New Testament. In other words they are translated from the Greek and Aramaic languages, that is, what the 1st century people spoke in. So the Greek New Testament is going to say the same thing for all of the translations.

Paul tells Timothy in 2 Tim. 2:15, "Be diligent to present yourself approved to God, a worker who doesn't need to be ashamed, correctly teaching the word of truth." In the King James it says to rightly divide the Word of God. The Greek understanding is to dissect, to cut a straight line. It gives us a picture of someone toiling over the Word of God and not adding or subtracting from it. Someone who has taken the time to understand what was being said to the ones that this letter was written to.

If we are going to divide the Word of God correctly we must take into account all of these factors before making a judgment what is being said and who is qualified, and who is not. The church over the years has done a lot of damage to people who were gifted by the Holy Spirit and seeking to do God's will in their lives.

At the same time, the church, has grieved the Holy Spirit by putting a stop to what He was doing. The Bible says that it is God who places people in the church, according to the gift that He has given them. Who are we to say no we can't use you, when it was God who put them there?

On the other side of the coin, I have seen churches that let people do the job of deacon, or even pastor, but they will not ordain them, or call them by those names. Is it the names or the job that is important? If that person is not qualified to do the job, then why are they doing it under an assumed title like yokefellow, or some other name to let them do what they are gifted at?

The word in the Greek for divorce never occurs in 1 Tim. 3, nor does it in Titus 1. The fact is that there are three Greek words used for divorce in the New Testament. One is found in Matt 5:32, the word is apostasion. We get our word apostasy from it, but in this case it means serve with a letter of divorcement. In this passage Jesus tells the Jewish leadership that God hates divorce, and He does, but He also hates sin in general. And here Jesus gives the exception for the rule, which in the case of adultery.

The second place we find a Greek word for divorce is in 1 Cor. 7:11. Paul here talks about if Christian married couple, both being Christians divorces they are to remain unmarried or go back together with each other. The Greek word used here is aphiemi, which means to put away, or divorce.

The third place is in 1 Cor. 7:15. This word is chorizo, which means to separate, to divide, to put asunder, or to divorce. Here Paul tells a Christian that if they are married to an unbeliever and the unbeliever does not want to stay with them to let them go, that they are not bound to them. The Greek understanding to be not bound to them is to be released from a covenant. They are free from the covenant of married. This is the same language used if a spouse dies and the one living is no longer bound to the covenant of married and is free to marry another.

None of these Greek words are used in 1 Tim. 3 or in Titus 1. The Greek word used there is mia, which means only one. Never any where in the New Testament is it used to refer to divorce, it means simply, only one. If we were to couple that understanding with the knowledge of the history of that area in the 1st century, we would find that the problem being addressed there was polygamy, not divorce. Paul is saying that pastors, and deacons, and church leadership ought not to be practicing polygamy.

This doesn't take away from the seriousness with which we ought to take divorce. Marriage is ordained from God and two people ought to enter into marriage with all seriousness, and intent of being married until death do they part, but we also must stick with the Biblical framework for the church and our relationships in the church, including ministry. If we are to say that we believe the Word of God to be inerrant and God's Word, then we also ought to be careful of how we use it to live by. And we most certainly ought to be careful as to how we apply it to others lives. We have caused great damage to people that have already been hurt over the years. It is time that we begin to mend the hurts that we have caused, and divide God's Word correctly.

CHAPTER 5

Coming Along Side

I don't know about you, but I have been in situations that I knew that I was speaking the truth to people, things that God laid on my heart, things that I knew they were suppose to hear, and had people just verbally lay me out like a dirty wash cloth. I remember how horrible that I felt, and even betrayed by those that I loved enough to tell them the truth about a situation they were in, that they shouldn't be in. At those times I had wished that I had some one that would come along side of me and help me up, and through those times.

I know that all of us have been through those times, and I know that all of us have felt very much the same way that I just described. So what do we do when those things happen, and what are we supposed to do for each other when these things happen? Does the Bible speak to these things? And where do I go to find it if it does?

The Bible does speak about these things but not in the way that you may think. The Bible tells us that we are to become like Christ in all we are and do. Most of us think about be loving and suffering for Christ, or as Christ suffered. We often think in terms of ourselves going through these things, and not what we are supposed to do when others go through these things.

We as a church have become very self centered in our thinking, and thus in our actions, we think in terms of ourselves, not those around us. This keeps us thinking and focusing on us and our problems, and never leads us to serve others and even think about what they are feeling and going through.

Jesus was not like this in any part of His life. In John 13:1-10 we find our Lord and Savior doing something that if we had been in the same situation we would never have thought of doing. Here is Jesus, who at this time knows what is about to happen to Him. He knows that within a few short hours He is to be arrested, beaten beyond recognition, and the next day nailed to a cross until He dies.

If that had been you or I the last thing we would have been thinking is about anyone else and what they needed. Let's be real, we would have been thinking on how to get out of the mess we were in. How can I get out of this, or at least escape without anyone noticing where I went?

That is not what Jesus is thinking though. Jesus is having a meal with His disciples, and instead of thinking of Himself, He gets up after supper and takes His clothes or outer robe off, puts on the clothing of a servant, and washes the feet of His disciples. He is the one who is about to face beatings, and death, and He is the one thinking about others, instead of wanting them to think about Him, He is thinking about them.

Wow! What a picture of total self abandonment for the sake of those He loved. But here it comes, the lesson that we are to get. In verse 14 of the same chapter, Jesus tells us what we are to be like. He says, "So if I, your Lord and Teacher, have washed your feet, you ought also to wash one another's feet." There it is, we are to follow in the foot steps of our Lord. We are to be concerned with each other over our own problems.

What does this have to do with coming along side of others? Everything, what are the reasons we use for not doing so. I would like to help others when they are going through struggles, but I have so many problems in my own life that I just don't have time. Or maybe, I am a little bit ashamed of the things they do, and I don't want to embarrass myself by siding with them. Or I don't want anyone to know that I am a Christian because it could cause me problems at work. Or I just wouldn't know what to tell them.

If we are going to follow the Bible, then we are going to have to make a decision about the priority of all of these things in our lives, turn to the Bible and decide what God's Word says about these things. Then we must make a decision as to whether we are going to believe and follow the Word of God. So what does God say about these things? We know by the verse that we just read in John 13 that we are to be like Jesus, because He said that we are to follow in His example.

Paraclete

We have talked about how that people in the Bible were named according to their characteristics. That is true of God as well. God revealed Himself to people in the Bible according to His nature and how He works in people's lives. God provided the sacrifice needed for Abraham, and Abraham came to know God is the God who provides.

The same is true of the rest of the Godhead as well. One of the names for the Holy Spirit is Paraclete. Paraclete means, one who speaks in favor of, intercessor, advocate, or legal assistant. This is important for us to understand, because this is the job that the Holy Spirit does for us.

The reason that I am pressing this so hard is this, because that is what the Holy Spirit does with us and that is what we are to allow the Holy Spirit to do with us and others. He will use us in these capacities to help others. We are to speak in favor of those that are brothers and sisters; we are to intercede for them when things are tough in their lives, and we are to be their advocate and stand up for them when they need our help.

That is what is coming along side of them. It is to put away our problems, or concerns, or time, and come along side of them and be with them through whatever they are going through, even when it might cause us problems, because people would get to know where we stand.

Think about this for a minute. I am not talking about when they are wrong just defending them as if they were right, they need to be corrected gently, or church discipline may be in order if they refuse to listen, but I am talking about those that are working their calling out in their life and are struggling with life as it is going. We are not to leave them for the wolves to devourer just because we are afraid of the wolves ourselves.

We are to come along side of them, and we are to defend them, and give them Biblical counsel that will encourage them to continue in the faith. We are to be on our knees interceding for them in our prayers. How many times have we told someone that we would be praying for them, and then walked away from them and forget to pray? We can't justify it by saying that we have a bad memory. We pray for those things that are dear to us. Does that mean that our brothers and sisters in the Lord are not dear to us? Think about it for a moment, and let's get real with ourselves, are they really a priority in our lives?

Jesus never forgets about us, and we hope that when we are in trouble and call our brothers and sisters that they don't just forget us in their prayers, we hope that they are not only praying for us, but we hope that they are pouring out their prayers for us and bringing it before the throne of God. That is what they are asking us to do when they call us and ask us to pray.

If we are to be disciple's of Christ, which is what we are to be according to the Scripture we just looked at, we could use this to measure our walk with the Lord. How do we measure up? In America we have gotten this it is all about me attitude that ought to cause us to humble ourselves before the Lord and bring us to a place of repentance. We need to take a hard look at ourselves, with the Bible as our measuring stick or rule and start getting serious about our walk with Him.

John 14:16, 26

In John 14:16 it says, "And I will ask the Father, and He will give you another Counselor to be with you forever." In the King James Version it says Comforter instead of Counselor. The importance of this is that the Word in the King James Version gives us a little clearer picture of what this means. The Word Comforter means to come along side of you. It also means to come to one's defense, but I want us to see this come along side of.

Think of it this way, if you had suffered a leg injury and you were having a difficult time standing up, or even getting up, you would need someone to come along side of you and hold you up, or give you the strength to stand and walk to where you needed to go. We have seen this in cowboy movies on T.V. where a cowboy gets shot and he has his partner come along side of him and help him to safety.

That is what the Holy Spirit does to us. He comes along side of us and gives us what we need. Strength when we are facing tough times, understanding when we don't see what's going on clearly, direction when we don't know which way to turn, and comfort when we can't seem to muster what it takes to continue.

This is closely tied to us as well. Who does the Holy Spirit use to do these things? Sure sometimes there is an inner strength that seems to come from no where, but He also uses the body to come along side of us and minister to us according to their gifts. This is called edifying the body, or building the body up in Christ.

In 1 Cor. 12:7 it says that the spiritual gifts are manifestations of the Holy Spirit. It is the Holy Spirit at work in the body to build the body up, or in this case to come along side of someone and help them through whatever they are going through, to encourage them with God's Word by reminding them what it says for their situation. This is spoken of in John 14:26, "But the Counselor, the Holy Spirit-the Father will send Him in my name-will teach you all things and remind you of everything I have told you."

Do you hear the work of the pastor, or a Sunday Scholl Teacher, or maybe just a mentor, someone who has built a special relationship with you. All this time you thought that they were really good at knowing what to say when in fact it was the Holy Spirit at work in them building you up just like Jesus said that He would.

Look at what it says in verse 16, it says that when Jesus asked for us to receive the Comforter, or Counselor that was what the Father would do. It didn't say that He might, or that He would think about it, it says He will. You are important to the Father through His Son Jesus Christ, and this is something that you can count on happening because He said that He would.

We ought to be seeing this happen all the time, and my guess is that we do see it happening much more that we think we do; we just didn't recognize who is doing the talking or the comforting. We thought it was the people we were with when in fact it was God at work through them to grow us up in Him.

How many times has God talked to us through another person and we just look at them as people, instead of looking at them as God using them? Think about the times that you may have taken what the pastor said lightly and not applied it to your life thinking that it was just from them, instead of from God? Is it kind of scary to think about? I mean to think back about the times that God has spoken and we haven't listened. Fortunately we serve a loving and merciful God who knows that we don't always understand what is going on around us, even when it is Him that is speaking to us.

All that is being said here is that we need to look at things more closely. We need to go to the Bible and try to understand what is being said here. We need to listen when the pastor teaches because God is using him to speak to all of us, or the Sunday School Teacher, or that person that loves us and doesn't what to see us walk away from God's plan for us.

John 15:26

How many time have you been in a situation that you were desperately looking for what way to go, or maybe how to understand a situation that you were in? The more that you tried to figure it out the more emotional stress you experienced. At that time you would have given anything to have someone come and be able to clear those things up for you.

Listen to John 15:26, "When the Counselor comes, the One I will send you from the Father-the Spirit of truth who proceeds from the Father-He will testify about me."

He is called the Spirit of Truth. We can know exactly what the Father has in mind for us and our situations. He wants us to know the direction that He wants us to travel, and the things that He wants us to do.

Listen to 1 Cor.2:15-16, "The spiritual person, however, can evaluate everything, yet he himself cannot be evaluated by anyone. For who has known the Lord's mind, that he may instruct Him? But we have the mind of Christ."

Here it is we have the mind of Christ. This is the Spirit of Truth that John spoke of that testifies of Christ. Jesus wants us to know all that there is to know about Him, but even more importantly He wants us to know Him, so He has put His mind in us through the indwelling of the Holy Spirit so that we have access to His mind and how He thinks in every situation we come into.

This is that testifying of Him, to know what He wants from us in each situation we are in, so that we can be obedient to Him in all situations in our lives.

This is the deepest coming along side of us that we can get. He comes along side of us from an indwelling standpoint. Understand this is also spoken of in Romans 8:26-27, "In the same way the Spirit also joins to help in our weaknesses, because we do not know what to pray for as we should, but the Spirit Himself intercedes for us with unspoken groaning. And He who searches the hearts knows the Spirit's mind-set, because He intercedes for the saints according to the will of God."

This is so cool, we don't know what to pray for, but the Holy Spirit searches our hearts and knows exactly what we need. He then intercedes for us to the Father, which knows the Spirit's mind, and answers the prayers.

The very Godhead is not only praying for us, but is also answering those prayers for us. And we come to know what He wants for us through His Word, prayer, and the church, or those we are in relationship with in the church.

We come to know what God wants for us, or the direction that we are to take, through God being at work in our lives. As we draw into a closer more intimate relationship with God, we get to know God more and more in our live. As that happens we get to know His mind and His desires for us.

Then our job, once we know these things is to be obedient to Him in all that He wants to do. We learn to line up with Him. Jesus did this as He said that He only does what He sees the Father doing, and He only says what He has heard the Father speak.

This is the intimacy that Scripture talks about. When we get married we start to learn what makes our spouses tick. In fact, we start to learn how they will respond to certain situations they come into contact with.

Sometimes when things happen we know how they will respond, and that affects us emotionally, good or bad. Sometimes we feel like we don't want to tell them something because we know how they are going to take it.

This is the same principle that Scripture is talking about here. He wants us to be able to get to know Him so intimately that we know what He is going to say and do about any situation. He also wants us to get to know Him so intimately that we know how He will treat us with mercy and grace, and how gentle He is toward us.

These are the same things that He wants us to learn and be able to come along side of others and do. We are not to just have that relationship with Him that is like this, but we are to have that kind of relationship with one another. We are His body the church, and we are to respond to one another the same as He does with us.

John 16:7

Jesus taught the disciples, just before He died and went to be with the Father, a lesson that we need to get here. This lesson is taught in John 16:7.

"Nevertheless, I am telling you the truth. It is for your benefit that I go away, because if I don't go away the Counselor will not come to you. If I go, I will send Him to you."

Jesus says that for Him to go it is a benefit for us. The truth is we all wish that Jesus had never gone, or that we had been born and lived when Jesus walked the earth. But Jesus is saying here that for Him to go becomes a benefit for us.

In the King James Version the word that is used instead of benefit is expedient. Expedient means to bring together, or what is helpful for us. He is saying that by going and sending the Comforter or the Counselor it will bring together what is good for us.

Why is it good for us? Because when we have the Holy Spirit that indwells us we will not need someone that we need to go and hunt up to answer our questions for us. That person will be with us all the time, because He lives in us as Christians.

We have someone that is with us, inside of us that has access to our minds, if we let Him he will guide us, and remind us of what Jesus said about any situation we face.

As we read the Word of God and put the Word of God into our minds, the Holy Spirit makes it come alive. We are able through Him to see how it applies to our lives. He shows us how it applies.

As we surrender to His leading He empowers us to apply it to our lives and we begin to live out the Word of God in our lives.

Psalm 32:8 says, "I will instruct you and show you the way to go; with my eye on you, I will give counsel." Here it is, the Father is going to instruct us and show us in the way that we are supposed to go. How does He do this? Through His Word, as the Holy Spirit shows us what His Word looks like when applied to our live.

This also happens as we are taught by pastors, teachers, evangelists, apostles and prophets. Going to church and learning from those that God has placed over us is part of the Holy Spirit growing us up in Him to the Stature of Christ so we won't be tossed here and there by every wind of doctrine that comes along, and so we will mature in Christ.

This is coming along side as the Scriptures describe it. This is what it looks like when we apply the Word of God to our lives. When we come along side of someone, it is really the Holy Spirit coming along side of them. And when we have someone else come along side of us it is God at work in our lives.

I am speaking of godly people coming along side of us, and using godly counsel, God's Word reminding us of what it says in His Word. So the next time you have someone come to you when you are down, or in some kind of difficult place and remind you of what Scripture says, don't get mad at them, it is the Holy Spirit coming along side of you, and it is for your benefit.

Instead of getting mad because they told you something you didn't want to hear, praise the Lord instead, knowing that He is seeking to be a benefit to you. He is trying to grow you up in Him, to keep you on solid ground and not let you slip away.

CHAPTER 6

Contentment

We live in a society that is anything but content. We hear about it on the news all of the time, and we read it in the newspapers that people are not content with their lives, nor are they content in the world around them.

I live in a small community and county and we have a newspaper that has a Letter to the Editor's section. People use this section to vent their entire discontentment about all that is going on in the world.

Here it is May of 2005 and people still haven't gotten over Bush being elected president. They write into the newspaper all of the time and talk about how Bush is doing this or doing that and that He never should have been elected in the first place.

I heard a section of the news on T.V. the other night that was saying that baby boomers are buying second homes. It says that they are looking for more income and using these second homes as income homes.

I have nothing against making money, but people can't seem to get enough of it, and they will do what ever it takes to make more of it. People that are selling drugs, many times got involved to make money.

I have heard people ask me if I was aware of how much money they could make selling drugs? The people that are using drugs started off using many different kinds because they were discontented in their lives.

They were discontented with their home lives when they were growing up, or they were discontented with their married lives and their spouses. Some of these were in bad shape in their homes, it is true, but they are looking for contentment in some part of their lives.

But we find that Christians are discontented with their walk with Christ. Many are blaming it on Christ Himself, saying that Christianity is not what it is cracked up to be. I have heard people come to me and tell me that they have tried Christianity and it did not work for them.

They are talking about Christ as if He were some drug that they have tried and it wasn't good enough for them, so they discarded Him as they would other things they have tried that didn't work.

The truth of the matter is that the way that they approached Christianity it is no surprise to me that it didn't work. The truth of the matter is that most of them never tried Christ, they tried religion instead. And that is what we are selling in church today many times.

True Christianity is not a religion to be tried with all of the other religions of the world trying to see which one is the most satisfying, and brings the most contentment. Anyone approaching Christianity from that frame of mind will find total discontentment.

Christianity is not a consumer product to be tried to see if it fits you. Christianity is a relationship with a living God, and just as with any relationship, as we try to find intimacy, we have to learn to be in that relationship with Him.

We have this weird sense about us that says that we are the consumers and that we are the ones that are to be looked up to and treated as if we had no problems. The truth of the matter is that we have a deadly problem, and Jesus is the only cure for our problem.

The reason that we are discontented with life is that we are not living this life the way that we were created to live it. And if we are to have contentment in this life it will be defined by the originator of life who is the Creator of the universe and everything in it.

Contentment isn't found in trying things hoping that at some point we will find what ever it is that satisfies us. Contentment comes as we learn to live the life that we were meant to live. And that can only come as we come into an intimate relationship with Jesus Christ, and the Father, through the Holy Spirit.

When we come into that relationship with Him, then we are at the beginning of our journey towards contentment. Contentment is something that we learn, not something that we just find in trying different things. Contentment has an object as the focus our contentment.

Philippians 4:11-13

This passage is one that we must understand, I believe, to come to the beginning of our contentment. In this passage we will see that it isn't things that bring contentment, it is a person.

"I don't say this out of need, for I have learned to be content in whatever circumstances I am. I know both how to have little, and I know how to have a lot. In any and all circumstances I have learned the secret of being content-whether well fed or hungry, whether in abundance or in need. I am able to do all things through Him who strengthens me."

Paul says here that contentment is something that he learned. It is important here for us to look at this. Paul isn't saying that by just going through things he happened to learn these things. The Greek word for learned, really means to be taught.

Paul is saying that he had been taught how to be content. He had to have someone teach him the lessons that he had learned. He has been taught these things as he has learned to put something into practice. There is a lesson plan that he was taught from so to speak.

Through this passage we are able to learn something about Paul's life, and through other passages. Paul did not always have everything he wanted, and even sometimes the things that we would think he needed.

It says that he didn't always have the food that he needed, or the money to buy things. But he does say that he knows how to have a little or a lot. The truth of the matter is that we don't always know how to do this.

Some of us would not know how to handle a large amount of money. I have heard people say that if they could just win the lottery they would be set. And I have heard about all of these people that have won the lottery that have gone bankrupt after they did. They did not know how to have a lot.

On the other hand, I know some people that have always had money, and plenty of it. If these people all of a sudden lost everything they had, they would not know how to make it with no money. They would just lie down and die.

Paul is saying that he has been taught to be a good steward of what he has whether it is a little or a lot. He has learned stewardship with whatever resources that the Lord provides him with.

Also we can see that Paul had a different focus than on those material things of this world. His focus was not on things but was on someone. Paul was focused on Christ. Paul was in love with Christ, and it was Christ that made Paul content, not things.

Do you remember when you were in love the first time? It didn't matter what was going on around you. It didn't matter how much food you ate, or how much money you had, the most important thing for you was to be around the one that you adored. Your focus was entirely on them. Most of the time you weren't even aware of all the things that had been going on around you. When you were with the one you loved nothing else mattered.

That is what Paul is saying. The secret to being content is not in things, even things that we need, it is in being in love with Christ. Paul had been ship wrecked, stranded, hungry, beaten, in prison, name it and it had happened to Paul. But Paul was in love, and nothing else mattered.

That is the secret. Once you know Christ and intimacy with Him, He becomes all things to you. That is the strength that Paul is talking about in this passage. And it is also the frame work for Matt. 6:33, "But seek first the Kingdom of God and His righteousness, and all of these things will be provided for you."

Paul found that he didn't have the strength to do anything, but if he stayed in Christ he had all of the strength that he would ever need.

1 Tim. 6:6-10

Not only was Paul's focus not on things here, Paul's whole reason for living had nothing to do with this life. Paul didn't consider himself a resident of this world or as the Bible would say of this cosmos, or this world system.

Paul's mind was on what lay ahead for him, not what he could get out of this world. Paul knew that the secret to life was that you use the things of this world to get, but you don't get attached to any of it. His attachment was something, someplace that was beyond this world, in fact, his concern was for a place that would out last this present age. Paul was focused and had his mind fixed on the heavenly.

Paul had this to say in Phil. 3:8, "More than that, I also consider everything to be a loss in view of the surpassing value of knowing Christ Jesus my Lord. Because of Him I have suffered the loss of all things and consider them filth, so that I may gain Christ".

Paul is talking here about what we have been talking about. Paul knew, at one time, what it was like to have all that he wanted. Paul was a Pharisee, and the next member of the Sanhedrin Counsel, the Jewish Counsel.

Paul thought at one time that He had arrived and gained all that one could gain in this life. Then Paul met Christ. From that point on Paul's idea of what was important changed for him.

Paul went from thinking that earthly gain and importance was important, to knowing that there was something that was eternal that could only be gained through a relationship with Jesus Christ.

Listen to what he says, all that he had he counts as loss. That word loss in the Greek means detriment. It means that all that this world has to offer will only serve to get in the way of this relationship with Christ if one focus' on that.

He goes on to say that knowing Christ Jesus has far greater value than anything that this world could ever produce. All that he had before he counts as filth, something to be removed, something that is disgusting. The only thing he wants is to get close to Christ.

And that is what he is saying in 1 Tim. 6:6-10, "But godliness with contentment is a great gain. For we brought nothing into the world, and can take nothing out. But if we have food and clothing we will be content with these. But those who want to be rich fall into temptation, a trap, and many foolish and harmful desires, which plunge people into ruin and destruction. For the love of money is a root of all kinds of evil, and by craving it, some have wandered away from the faith and pierced themselves with many pains."

Some today say that they are seeking spirituality, and they think that that will get them contentment and happiness. Paul doesn't use the word spirituality here, and for a good reason I believe. Spirituality could mean many different things. Looking to places other than God for spirituality. Demons are spirits too, and one can find themselves being spiritual bound to them.

Paul uses the term godliness; this is a total different term. This term says that someone is seeking after God, not spirits. People seeking after godliness are seeking to please God not themselves. Many people who are seeking after spirituality are seeking to find inner peace through worldly means. Some forms of meditation are these things.

But here Paul is talking about making your focus, your goal to be what God wants you to be, not want you want for yourself. Then he goes on to talking about the truth of our situation. The world's goods are just for today, or this life.

When we came into this world we brought nothing with us, and when we leave we can't take anything from this world with us. The only thing that we will be able to take with us is our relationship with Jesus Christ.

When we die that is what will be important. It won't be about how much money you had in this life, or how many houses you had, or how many toys you had and were able to use. It will be about whether you knew Jesus or not.

Paul goes on to say that if we have food and clothing then that is enough and we ought to be content in these things. He is not saying that having these things is wrong, but he is saying that if our heart is after these things we are not in the right place.

He says that those that seek after riches are placing themselves in a place that will cause them to have temptations that are not necessary for them to go through. It is placing a trap of their own hands for them to be caught by.

Can you imagine having a huge rat trap, setting it for yourself so that you can trap yourself with it? Most of us would say that is silly, but that is what Paul is saying here.

But he doesn't stop there. Paul goes on to tell us that it will cause us to be plunged into ruin and destruction. Most of us would say that if I don't have money I will be plunged into ruin and destruction. But Paul isn't concerned with the loss of worldly things; he is concerned with the loss of a relationship with Christ.

Paul still goes on, and he tells us that the love of money is the root of other kinds of evil as well. Paul says that if we love money we are susceptible to falling away from the faith. This is about our walk and intimacy with Christ.

We have all seen these things happen to someone we know. It may not have been money per say, but it most certainly had to do with things. I have seen people do this with jobs. Before they had this job their whole focus was to be all that they could be in Christ. When they got the job their whole concern was to be all that they could be on the job. They even quit coming to church as much as they used to until finally they quite coming at all.

I talked to them when this started to happen, and they told me that there was a great demand on them at work, and they had to have this job because they needed to make a living. The more demands that the job put on them the less they were interested in work.

Whenever I saw them they would tell me how great they were doing at work, how they had gotten raises and the whole thing. Funny thing is that they never told me that they were getting closer to Christ. The honest ones told me they had been suffering in their relationship with Christ.

We can see this happen with Lot's wife. When God destroyed Sodom and Gomorrah, God told Lot to flee the city. Lot took his wife and daughter's and took off. But not all of them made it out of the city. Lot's wife had a fondness for the city and was turned into a pillar of salt.

It says in Genesis 19:26, "But his wife looked back and became a pillar of salt." She didn't want to get destroyed with the rest of the city, but her heart was fond of the city and it destroyed her with the city.

That was not Paul's relationship with the Lord though. Listen to what he says in Phil. 1:21-22, "For me, living in Christ and dying is gain. Now if I live in the flesh, this means fruitful work for me; and I don't know which one I should choose."

Here is Paul thinking out loud about whether it is better to live or to die. To live for him is to be fruitful in the work of the Lord. But equally important to him is to die and be with the Lord. Paul is torn by this decision.

Most of us would not have this problem at all. We would say there is no decision for me. I want to live, I have a lot of things that I am not through doing yet, and if we were to write down on a piece of paper what those things would be heavenly things would be at the bottom of our list.

Peter even said it like this in 1 Peter 2:11, "Dear friends, I urge you as aliens and temporary residents to abstain from fleshly desires that war against you."

Peter is saying that we do not belong here permanently. The word alien in the Greek means living here as someone who does not have the right of citizenship here. Don't bind yourself down with the worldly concerns and the material things that cause you to forget you are not here forever.

The secret of contentment lies in our relationship with Jesus Christ and a proper understanding of who we are in Christ. Peter also tells us that we belong to the Kingdom of God that is where our citizenship is. And He tells us not to live like those that don't have citizenship in the Kingdom of God.

Being content comes when we fall in love with Jesus Christ and desire to be with Him more than we desire anything else in this world. When the things of this world no longer mean anything to us, and we are just happy with doing His will.

Romans 15:13

Now we need to look at this further. The definition to be contented implies that there is a joy and a peace involved in our emotional and mental state. If I am to be content, I am said to be at peace, my life has a certain joy about it.

This is what people around the world are looking for. In fact people in general do not have this contentment that brings with it joy and peace. To prove that look at the drug market today. I don't just mean illegal drugs I am talking about prescription drugs. These are drugs that doctors are giving people to make them feel more at peace with themselves and the world around them.

The truth of the matter is these drugs do not make them feel at peace, but instead they make their emotions flat where they don't feel anything at all, and they walk around like an emotional zombie if you will.

Even with the drugs there is not joy and peace that go along with their emotional state at best they just don't feel the things that are being done to them. And some prefer to have this over the feeling of unrest and fear of life.

So when the Bible speaks of this, how is it done? If the Bible says that it can be done then we are supposed to be able to live this out in our lives, wouldn't you agree? And that is exactly what the Bible is saying that we can have.

Let's look at Romans 15:13, "Now may the God of hope fill you with all joy and peace in believing, so that you may overflow with hope by the power of the Holy Spirit."

First of all we need to see that hope isn't something that we just have, nor is it something that we can obtain on our own. This passage says that the source of hope is God.

If we want to have hope in this world we must turn to God. It is only through God that one can have hope. Do you need hope? We all need hope. Without hope, people have committed suicide, fallen into drug addiction, and alcoholism.

Think about this for a minute, people have tried all kinds of things to find hope. They have sought after money and things, so they would have hope for the future. And they have found that money and things couldn't bring them hope.

But here it is in God's Word, God is the source of hope, there is no other source, if you want hope, you must turn to God to obtain it. Some may say, I have turned to God and I still am not content, joyful, and peaceful.

Well there is more to this verse that we must look at. Second, we find joy and peace in believing in God. This is putting our trust in Him. This is the only way that we are able to live the Christian life. We cannot please God without faith that is what the Bible says.

The Bible says that the righteous are to walk by faith. This is a total trust in God for all that we have. This means that I trust in what God says, and I trust God with my entire life and everything in it. I trust Him in every circumstance in my life.

To trust God this way means that in every situation I will turn to God and His Word, and I will stand on His Word in every situation, no matter what it looks like, and I will trust God to carry out in my life the things that He has promised He would.

Look at the third things it says. If we will do that the Holy Spirit will empower us to live this life with the contentment, joy, and peace that we have been talking about to this point.

The contentment that we read about in the Bible is not something that is common to this world, nor is it something that can be obtained in this world. The contentment, joy, and peace that we are talking about is a supernatural empowerment from God.

Do you want that in your life? If you do then it is about turning to God, repenting of your sins of unbelief, and putting your trust in God, and asking Him to fill you with that hope that only comes from Him.

CHAPTER 7

Listening

It is vitally important for people to be in the Word of God. Daily Bible Study is a discipline that we all need to develop in our lives. This is what God is saying to us and we are able to see, not about God, but what God says that we need.

Listening is all part of this discipline. Some think that they will mature by reading God's Word daily, but it goes much deeper than that. It takes more than just poring over the Scripture to truly receive life, or the abundant life that Jesus came to give us.

In John 5:39, Jesus tells the Jewish leaders, "You pore over the Scriptures because you think you have eternal life in them, yet they testify about me." Jesus was saying that He is life, and if we want to have life, the changed life, we must come into a relationship with Him that is both intimate and growing.

To have this relationship we must not only know about Him, but we must come to a place in our relationship with Him where we begin to listen to Him, and apply what we hear. Application is paramount to our continued growth.

Unfortunately, many people are doing the same thing as the Pharisee's did. They pore over the Scriptures and think that something miraculous is going to happen. They go to church and they listen to the sermon and walk out thinking what a wonderful message that they have heard, and yet that is all the affect that it had on them.

To listen is something different that we understand if it is going to change us the way that Scripture says it will. Have you ever wondered why something that the Scripture said wasn't working in your life? It is because we think in today's society that listening is a passive thing. But that is not what the Word of God says about listening. According to God's Word listening is active.

Mark 4:3-9

In Mark chapter 4 we find an example of this being told to a very large crowd according to the Scripture. "Listen! Consider the sower who went out to sow. As he sowed, this occurred: Some seed fell along the path, and the birds came and ate it up. Other seed fell on rocky ground where it didn't have much soil, and it sprung up right away, since it didn't have deep soil. When the sun came up, it was scorched, and since it didn't have a root, it withered. Other seed fell among thorns, and the thorns came up and choked it, and it didn't produce a crop. Still others fell on good ground and produced a crop that increased 30, 60, 100 times what was sown. Then He said, Anyone who has ears to hear should listen!"

Here we are with several things we must look at. First is that the seed spoken of here is the Word of God. And the different types of soil are in reference to the way the Word of God is received. Jesus starts off by telling His hearers to Listen! This word in the GK means to perceive what is being said with understanding. Jesus said that we are to listen with the intent to understand.

This kind of listening is not passive. To listen this way is to be seeking to understand. I remember very clearly when I was going to school. I remember reading theology from people that had written works that were deep. It was very important that I understand what was being said because I had to write a paper on it and be tested on this material.

I worked hard at trying to understand what was being said. I went over the same paragraph a number of times sometimes so that I could grasp what the depth of the passage and what the writer was trying to say. I even went to dictionaries to find out the meanings of certain words that they used.

I was determined to understand completely the lesson that I had been given. I not only wanted to understand it but I also wanted to be able to teach it and explain it to others, and speak with clarity.

That is what is being said here to the people that Jesus is speaking to. The rocky soil, the road side seed, and the seed that fell among the thorns were people that didn't go after what Jesus said with this intensity. They just heard with their ears and not seeking with their hearts. Jesus wants the heart involved, not just the ears.

On the other hand, those that produced 30, 60, 100 times the amount sown were people that did listen to Jesus with that kind of intensity. They sought what He was talking about, and they had a hunger in their being after His Word.

Mark 4:10-12

Did you know that Jesus wants you to know and understand all that He has said? But He isn't going to just give it to just anybody, He wants those that have a desire after Him.

Look at verses 10-12 of chapter 4 of Mark, "When He was alone with the Twelve, those who were around Him asked Him about the parables. He answered them, "The secret of the kingdom of God has been granted to you, but those outside, everything comes in parables so that they may look and look, yet not perceive; they may listen and listen, yet they might turn back-and be forgiven."

First of all, when it says that the Twelve asked Him the secret it was more than just asking in passing. The Greek word for asked also means that they had a desire to know. They wanted with all of their hearts to know the truth of the parables.

Second, Jesus told them that they had been granted to know the secret of the parables. Now remember, these parables were stories that were not real stories, but their purpose was to relay truth to people that they would not be able to know any other way.

The key is that they were told by Jesus that they had been granted to know the truth. That is important for us to know, because it has been granted to us to know the truth about it as well.

The secret is that He wants us to listen with that desire that the Twelve had. That desire that comes from the heart that means more to you than life itself because it has to do with your relationship with Jesus which is your life.

Jesus goes on to describe those that didn't understand, and He says that they looked and yet they did not perceive. They looked as in passing, they looked just precursory look, just a surface scan, not wanting to do anything more than they absolutely had to.

This is the kind of look that one takes at something when they are too busy or preoccupied with something else. And these people most likely were there for other reasons. They followed Him and listened to Him because they loved to see His miracles.

They weren't interested in a relationship with Him that said that they had to do anything. How many Sundays have we gone to church hoping that we would receive a blessing there and get emotionally charged up? We all do this from time to time, and I for one love to get that emotional high that comes from being in the presence of God.

The truth is that we ought to be coming to church to listen, to seek after Him, to want to get to know Him better, and we ought to be willing to do whatever it takes to get closer to Him. We ought to desire what He wants us to do for Him, not what He can do for us.

When we come with that attitude, we find ourselves not only getting emotionally charged, but we find ourselves growing in Him, learning what we are to do for Him and His Kingdom.

In Matt. 7:7-8 it says, "Keep asking, and it will be given to you. Keep searching, and you will find. Keep knocking, and the door will be opened to you. For everyone who asks receives, and the one who searches finds, and to the one who knocks, the door will be opened."

The first part of verse 7 says to keep asking, and that is what the Greek says, it is a continual asking, and a continual knocking, and a continual searching that gets answered, and the door gets opened to, and finds what they are seeking from God.

Sometimes we go to a friend's house and we make three knocks on the door, and if our friend doesn't come to the door we assume they are not home and we leave.

What Jesus is saying is to keep knocking until He opens the door for you. Don't stop, keep knocking, keep knocking on His door until He comes and opens it to you.

When you loose your car keys and you are in a hurry to get some place, you don't just look through the house once and then call the people you were suppose to meet and tell them you can't make it do you?

No you tare up the house until you find those keys, and you do everything you can to get to where you are going. That is the kind of searching and seeking that He is looking for.

Do you remember when you were young and you wanted to do something? You would go to you parents and you would keep asking them for it until they finally gave in and let you go, or gave you what you wanted. That is the kind of asking that He is looking for.

Let's make one more thing clear here. He is not telling us to do this for just the things that we want, what He is saying here is that we are to be seeking Him and asking Him for that relationship with Him, and searching for His will.

When we do this we also start finding out all of those things that we were not able to know before, things that we had been asking Jesus about, and yet not seeking Him with all of ourselves. Even though it had been important to us, it was not the most important thing to us.

When we are after Him like this, then other things begin to happen in our lives. We start being the people that we are suppose to be, that He created us to be. And we will see this in the next section of Mark 4.

Mark 4:21-32

In Verses 13-20, Jesus begins to explain to the disciples what the parables mean. He explains that the seed is the word of God that gets proclaimed, and the different types of soil is really the way those that were given the seed listen and judged it necessary for their lives.

This has to do with what people think is important and what place they put these teaching in their lives. This is just what we have been talking about, is it something that we need, or is it something that we think is nice but not a necessity? What place does it take in your life?

Verses 21-32 has to do with what it looks like when it does take first place in your life. Jesus is saying that we can't get along by saying that it takes first place in our lives. We can't just mouth the words, if it really takes first place in our lives it will show.

Let's look at this closer, starting with verses 21-25. He also said to them, "Is a lamp brought in to be put under a basket or under a bed? Isn't it to be put on a lampstand? For nothing is concealed except to be revealed, and nothing is hidden except to come to light. If anyone has ears to hear, he should listen!" Then He said to them, "Pay attention to what you hear. By the measure you use, it will be measured and added to you. For to the one who has, it will be given, and from the one who does not have, even what he has will be taken away."

The seed, if taken into ones life, and applied to ones situation will produce something. In this case Jesus says that it will produce light. One important aspect of light is that when it is turned on you can see it.

If someone listens to the Gospel and takes it in you will be able to see the light shine from that person's life. It will change that person, and the change will be evident, so much so that that change will be able to be seen through that person. There will be a light emanating from that persons life.

Remember in 1 John chapter 1, John said that Jesus is the light, and anyone who belongs to Christ will walk in the light with Him, and that it will bring fellowship with the brethren.

The person who receives the seed of the Gospel into their life, and makes it a priority of their life will have a light that shines from them that will cause others to see the change in him or her. The Gospel will be proclaimed from them both in word and in deed.

Then Jesus goes on to say that there will be nothing that is held in secret that will not be revealed, and that all will come to light. Jesus is saying that if we watch and know what we are looking for we can tell where a person is at spiritually by looking at their lives.

How many times have we wondered where someone was at spiritually? According to Scripture we can discern the spiritual by what they are producing in their lives. If someone has truly made this commitment, then their lives will show the commitment that they made, there will be fruit that shows in their lives.

There will also be fruit that is produced when someone hasn't accepted Jesus as Lord and Savior, but the fruit there is different from the fruit of Salvation. We can see these different kinds of fruit in Gal. chapter 5.

Verses 22-23 in Gal. 5 are the fruits of the Spirit, and we have talked about this before, but here they are, love, joy, peace, patience, kindness, goodness, faith, gentleness, self-control. But here are the fruits of the flesh, sexual immorality, moral impurity, promiscuity, idolatry, sorcery, hatred, strife, jealousy, and outbursts of anger, selfish ambitions, dissensions, factions, envy, drunkenness, carousing, and anything similar.

These are the things that show who we belong to. They are the things that show what we are made of, and these are the things that Jesus is talking about in this passage of Scripture.

We don't have to spend our whole lives being fooled by the deceptive people in the world, but more importantly these are things that we ought to be measuring our own lives by to see if we measure up to the faith. These areas in our lives can show us the areas of our lives that are still unsurrendered to the Holy Spirit's control.

Jesus then says that what He has given us needs to be used for Him or we will run the chance of losing it. This is something that we need to look at carefully. Because it is important for us to know that others can tell when things are not right with us, even when we say that they are. Granted, it can only be discerned by someone who is themselves spiritual, but when you are not walking in the light you won't recognize the ones that are spiritual yourselves.

Mark 4:26-29

To listen is to be aware of what is going on around us. This is part of discernment, or being spiritual. We hear a lot about people being so spiritual today; it really has become a buzz word in today's society. I hear people say that so and so is so spiritual, and when I ask them what they are talking about they become very vague and are not really sure how to answer that question.

What they really mean is that so and so is mysterious, or mystical in the way they act. They are able to philosophize. Interestingly enough most of the people that I have talked to have no idea what the person is saying it just sounds deep, so therefore they must be spiritual.

That is not the Biblical definition of spiritual, and it most certainly isn't what will help you understand the word of God, and His plan for you. If we want to know about God we must first come into a relationship with Him where we are able to have His Spirit within us. Then we must come to a place where we can listen to what He is saying and then we are able to discern.

In this passage Jesus is talking about a farmer that is sowing seed on the ground. Jesus says that there is a lot that the farmer may not know as far as how the seed turns into a plant, but he does know that if he plants a field that within a period of time there will be a harvest that comes.

Also Jesus says that the farmer is not the one who produces the growth of the harvest, he just planted the seed, and he knows that it will somehow grow into a crop that he can harvest.

We are to listen to this and understand, be spiritual in our understanding. We are to plant the seed, and leave the results to Him, knowing that He will cause growth to happen, and have faith that there will be a harvest at the end.

Sometimes it is easy to get our eyes on the results that we want to see immediately, and when it doesn't happen immediately we loose hope and give up. Jesus tells us that the way to be victorious over hopeless is to listen and believe that things will happen the way that He says they will.

This means to stay at the task, don't lose heart, He will do what He says that He will, and in the end we will see His Kingdom that was harvest through the diligent sowers of the seed, His Word.

Being spiritual is different than the world's view of spiritual. To be spiritual is to be in tune with God through His Son Jesus Christ by coming into a right relationship with Him, and listening what He is saying in His Word, and putting that into practice in our lives.

Mark 4:33-34

We need to get this here as the Bible explains what Jesus was doing. It says that Jesus didn't talk to people without saying things in parables. He didn't speak to people that didn't belong to Him in any other way than in parables.

We need to listen carefully here. Some of the people that Jesus spoke to in parables were His people, they heard Jesus convey truth through parables, and upon hearing them they didn't understand them either.

It is important to Jesus that we are able to understand what He says to us. Look, when the people were gone, and He was alone with His disciples, Jesus explained to them what they meant. Jesus explained the truth of the parables to His own.

It is those that are willing to listen and do that He will reveal the truth to, and to guide us in the ways that He has for us. It is a heart issue. Where is your heart? If your heart is with the world, and all you want to see is the miracles that He does, there is a good chance you will miss the truth of the situation in your life. And you want Him above all else than this world has to offer, then you are the one that He will reveal the truth to. If your heart is after Him, He will reveal Himself and His purpose and direction for your life.

If you want to know Him above all else and take the time to be alone with Him, to you He will reveal the truth of the parables of your life. But you have to be after Him, and be willing to listen intently for want He wants to say to you with a willingness to carryout whatever He tells you.

We can see this in Luke 10:38-42, "While they were traveling, He entered a village, and a woman named Martha welcomed Him into her home. She had a sister named Mary, who also sat at the Lord's feet and was listening to what He said. But Martha was distracted by her many tasks, and she came up and asked, Lord, don't you care that my sister has left e to serve alone? So tell her to give me a hand. The lord answered her, Martha, Martha, you are worried and upset about many things, but one thing is necessary. Mary has made the right choice, and it will not be taken away from her."

Here is Martha thinking that she is doing the right thing by working and serving, but in reality she is about doing her own thing. Sometimes it is easier to do things than it is to wait and listen to what Jesus is saying.

In this case and in our case what it reveals is our lack of relationship with the Lord. He is the most important thing, and what He has to say is of vital importance, and if we miss that we will miss everything.

Mary had chosen the right thing and that was to set at Jesus' feet and soak in everything Jesus had to say. She wasn't worried or concerned about anything else other than what Jesus had to say. It is like she knew that what He had to say was the very thing she needed to carryout the task that she would be given later.

Jesus tells Martha that she is worried and upset. These are strong terms and indicate that she was focused on everything but what Jesus had to say about what was important. Martha had an agenda of her own and was put out when everyone else didn't fit into her agenda. Mary wanted Jesus' agenda.

This is the essence of listening. It is listening with the heart, knowing that what we hear from Jesus will be the most important thing we will ever hear in life, in fact, it is our life.

CHAPTER 8

The Laws that Govern Our Churches

The Jews had taken the 10 commandments that God gave Moses, and turned those laws into 860 laws that define those laws. They decided that what God had given Moses was not enough so they made laws to define the 10 commandments.

We have all heard about Phariseism, this is where people are so involved with the laws and rules that they forget what the original intent of the laws were about in the first place.

We have done this to some extent in our churches today. We look at what everyone else is doing, and we look at whether someone is following the rules or not.

We are, sometimes, more concerned with what people are doing than we are in having an intimate relationship with Jesus and with each other. And these two items are closely connected in our lives, more so than we realize most of the time. If we knew how closely they were related, we wouldn't have some of the difficulties we do with others, because we would seek to mend our relationships.

In 1 John 1:5-10 it says, "Now this is the message we have heard from Him and declare to you: God is light, and there is no darkness in Him. If we say, we have fellowship with Him, and walk in darkness; we are lying and are not practicing the truth. But if we walk in the light as He Himself is in the light, we have fellowship with one another, and the blood of Jesus His Son cleanses us from all sin. If we say, we have no sin, we are deceiving ourselves, and the truth is not in us. If we confess our sins, He is faithful and righteous to forgive us our sins and to cleanse us from all unrighteousness. If we say, we have not sinned, we make Him a liar, and His word is not in us."

Now let us look at what this says about our relationship with God, and our relationship with one another. This passage starts off by saying that God is light, and that there is no darkness in Him.

The word "light" in the GK is phos and means a lamp, or a torch. We can determine that God has no sin in Him but that is really not the thrust of this message. The meaning is that God is a lamp or torch that eliminates all dark places exposing all that is in the dark.

This means that He, when we come into contact with Him, will expose all that is in our hearts that has been in the past kept in secret. All of the sin we have not let anyone else see.

We, most often, do not let others see our hearts; we want them to only see those things that would make us look good to others. Well, God, when we come into contact with Him exposes those things. The idea here is that if we continue to walk in that light, we will be able to have fellowship with God.

This is the essence of confession and repentance. We are exposed to Him as we come to Him, and we see what is there the way He sees it, we agree with Him about the exact nature and condition of our hearts, and then ask Him to forgive us of that sin that is there.

He shows us the condition of our hearts. That is a very uncomfortable place to be, and sometimes it is so uncomfortable, and is so dirty for us to look at, we are not willing to admit what condition we are really in, so we pull away. Often times, not only do we pull away, but we point out others condition so we think it will take the light off of us.

By doing this we pull away from God and it says that we don't and can't have fellowship with Him. When that happens all that we do from that point becomes religious practice and nothing more. We no longer are in an intimate relationship with Jesus.

The result of this is that we can't have a relationship with one another as well. Sin does not just affect us; it also affects those around us as well. That is why when we practice sin, we offend God first, but we also affect those around us.

When we walk in the light with God, allowing Him to constantly expose the truth about us, we are also able to walk in a close relationship with each other. Others will be able to see the truth about us, and seeing how that Jesus has cleansed us, others will be able to see the grace of God.

A Look at the laws

You may ask what all of this has to do with the laws that govern our churches, and I say everything. It is those laws that will speak to others about where we are in our relationship with Jesus.

When we make laws of the church, what we are saying is that these are the things that are important to us. So important are these things that we are expecting everyone who becomes a part of this church to abide by them.

Having said that, it is important that we make the laws that govern our church to be laws that expose the heart of Jesus. The only way this is possible is if we make our governing laws based on God's Word and His Love for His people.

I know that I spoke of Love earlier in this book, but I would like to take another look at it in this chapter as well. It is love that we must use to govern our churches by, but not the love of the world, but the love of God.

The love of this world says that we can do whatever we please and that we ought to be allowed to do so. They would say anything short of that is not love. Yet they give a mixed message because they use some laws for their organizations that put restrictions on people.

The worlds love is a warm fuzzy feeling that can change whenever the feelings change. The worlds love leaves people lonely and confused about love, it says to some you are loved because of the way you dress, or the people you know and hang out with, or by your physical features.

God's love doesn't change and it has nothing to do with any of these things, but God is very specific about how His love ought to be applied to all situations, and it is that in which I would like to take a closer look at.

God's Love

To take a look at God's Love we will start in 1 Cor. 13. With God's love there are things that we think ought to show His love that have nothing to do with it.

1 Cor. 13:1-3 says, "If I speak the languages of men and of angels, but do not have love, I am sounding gong or a clanging cymbal. If I have the gift of prophecy and understand all mysteries and all knowledge, and have all faith, so that I can move mountains, but do not have love, I am nothing. And if I donate all of my goods to feed the poor, and give my body to be burned, but do not have love, I gain nothing."

We have all heard people use this text as a proof text for tongues, and unfortunately by doing this they have missed a vital passage dealing with godly love.

Paul is stressing a very important point to the church at Corinth here. There were some that were trying to prove their spirituality and their love for God by saying, Look at me; I perform all of these great signs and wonders. I speak in tongues,

I give to the poor, and look at my faith, no other has such faith as I do. This will prove my relationship with God.

Paul in this passage refutes what they are saying to people. He is saying you can do all those things that you want to do, but in the end you are no better than anyone if these things are not practiced from a heart of love for one another and for people.

Corinth was a place that each major cult from the known world at that time had a temple and a place of worship. The city was as corrupt as they come. For a woman to be called a Corinthian girl was the same thing as calling her a prostitute.

What Paul was saying is this, you can practice all of these things that you call spiritual you want to, and if it isn't motivation by a heart of love you are no different than the pagans around you.

They used gongs and cymbals in some of the pagan temples in that area to summons their gods into the building. So anything that we do that is not motivated by love is no different than any pagan practice in the world.

So, spirituality is not based on practice of things we think are spiritual, but it is based on love, and not the love of the world, but on a godly love. This is love that example God's love for us. So let us take a look at this kind of love.

Once again in 1 Cor. 13:4-8, "Love is patient; love is kind. Love does not envy; is not boastful; is not conceited; does not act improperly; is not selfish; is not provoked; does not keep a record of wrongs; finds no joy in unrighteousness, but rejoices in the truth; bears all things, believes all things, hopes all things, endures all things. Love never ends......".

Interestingly enough Paul starts off with telling us that love is produced by the Spirit. You may ask where he says that, and I would say look in Gal. 5:22-23 and you will find the fruits of the Spirit there. Then look at love and match up what love is and what the fruits of the Spirit are.

So what Paul is saying this, just because you do these practices does not make you spiritual. The truly spiritual person will produce in their life, or he will exhibit in his or her life the characteristics of the Holy Spirit.

Paul tells us in 1 Cor. 12:7, that these things are actually the Holy Spirit manifesting Himself through the person that is submitting to Him. Love is God at work through us.

Now let us look at another passage that describes what love is. 1 John 3:16 says, "This is how we have come to know love: He laid His life down for us. We should lay our lives down for our brothers."

We are able to see Jesus' love for us in the act that He performed on the cross. He gave His life as a ransom for us. He died for us, and we ought to lay our lives down for each other.

This doesn't necessarily mean that I have to physically die for my brother, although that may happen, but what it does mean is that I need to consider my brother over myself.

I need to make my brothers needs more important than my own. That is laying your life down for your brother. And that is the measurement that I am to use to govern the church.

When we allow other things to control the reasons we have for the governing laws of our church, according to this passage, we are no better that the pagan church that is around us. These are the places we are warning people to stay away from.

The problem is, if we are telling others to stay away from those places, maybe we ought to include ourselves in that list if love is not our tool of measurement.

CHAPTER 9

Spiritual Discernment

Today, we live in a world that takes great pride in appearances, and the accomplishments of people. They seek certain people to run the departments in the work place, based on the education, and also their appearance.

They are looking for people that will attract others and seem motivated so others will be motivated to accomplish company goals and direction that they would like to head in.

Unfortunately the church has begun to do some of the same things that the world does in choosing those that are to lead their churches. They make decisions about who will pastor their churches based on age, appearance and motivation.

That is not the way God chooses the man for His church. We can see this when God lead Samuel to Jesse to check out his sons for who would be Israel's next king. Samuel looked at how strong they looked, and how impressive each of Jesse's sons appeared.

The problem was that none of the sons that Samuel had chosen was the one that God had chosen. God told Samuel no to all of the sons that Samuel had seen. In fact, the man that God choose didn't look anything like the ones that had been chosen by Samuel. He was small and ruddy the Bible tells us, and wasn't anything that looked like a king.

God gave Samuel a very valuable lesson that day. God told Samuel that the way He selected people had to do with the heart and not outward appearances at all. He didn't pick him by age because David was just a kid.

This was Israel's second experience with a king that wasn't the one that God chose. Remember Saul? Saul was Israel's first king and was chosen the same way that Samuel tried to pick their new king. We know how that ended up. It was a disaster that lasted for a great portion of Israel's history. My suggestion to you is to go to 1 Samuel and read through Israel's history at that time.

God wants us to choose His man for the job of leading His church. And He is still concerned that we do things His way, not ours. This means that we are to be able to discern who that man is.

One of the ways to choose God's man God's way is through His Word, as we have discussed earlier in this book. We are to take a look at 1 Timothy 3 and see the qualifications for God's man for the job. We will find out that this has nothing to do with age or appearances.

The man God chooses is to be above reproach, devoted to his one wife, self controlled, sensible, respectable, hospitable, a good teacher, someone not addicted to wine, he must be gentle, and he can not be quarrelsome, not greedy, able to mange his household, and able to manage his family.

None of this has anything to do with outward appearances that would tend to draw a crowd, or to be a crowd pleaser for that matter. It has everything to do with the man's heart. If you were to look at the qualifications for pastor, you would see that they are characteristics, not outward at all. And if you were to really look closely at all of this you would be able to see that they have more to do with the Holy Spirit than anything else. That is because these are the fruits of the Spirit.

It is important for us to know this because that is what we are going to be talking about in this section. We are to be discerners of the Spirit, and not just lookers of outward things.

First John 4:1 tells us this, " Dear friends, do not believe every spirit, but test the spirits to determine if they are from God, because many false prophets have gone out into the world".

First, the scripture tells us not to believe every spirit. This tells us that there are other spirits out there and they will lie to us. We also know that Jesus Himself called Satan the father of all lies. He will send his spirits, or demons out there to lie to us so that we will be deceived and not do what God is truly leading us to do.

God never leaves us on our own, unable to know the truth. God in this same passage tells us to test the spirits. The word test in the Greek means to examine, or to scrutinize the spirits. But it goes on to say to recognize it as genuine after careful examination.

Just as it tells us to examine the spirits, we are to examine them according to the Word of God. Amazingly enough the word Bible means measuring stick, so we are to measure the spirits according to the Word of God.

At this point you may wonder what part of the Scripture we are to use. Use Gal. 5:16-26 where it tells us the fruits of the Spirit verses the fruits of the flesh. Use 1 Timothy 3:1-9 that tells us the characteristics of the pastor and his wife. In fact use 1 Timothy 2:15 where Paul exhorts Timothy to divide the Word of God correctly.

These are some of the measurements that need to be used to test the spirits. But also test the spirits within you and in the group selecting a pastor to see if all are willing to use those measurements to test the spirits.

Some people are really not qualified to be on a pastor search committee because they want to choose a pastor according to the flesh. Paul talks about this in Romans 8:6-8, "For the mind set of the flesh is death, but the mind set of the Spirit is life and peace. For the mind set of the flesh is hostile to God because it does not submit itself to God's law, for it is unable to do so. Those whose lives are in the flesh are unable to please God."

Those that are in the flesh are not to be on committees that appoint positions of leadership because they are thinking in the flesh, and they will make decisions based on flesh not the Spirit. So all must be examined to see if all are willing to test the Spirits according to God's Word, and not to fleshly standards.

The Greek here is talking about a mind set. We hear about peoples mind set all of the time. I hear some come to me and tell me that they have a mind set and they are too old, and have had this mind set for too long to change now.

Think about this! If they have that mind set, and if they are not going to change, is that really someone that we would want making choices for our leadership in the church?

We would do well to find those that are seeking the Lord's mind on these matters. Listen to what the Bible says on this matter in 1 Corinthians 2:14-16, " But the natural man does not welcome what comes from God's Spirit, because it is foolishness to him; he is not able to know it since it is evaluated spiritually. The spiritual person, however, can evaluate everything, yet he himself cannot be evaluated by anyone. For who has known the Lord's mind, that they may instruct Him? But we have the mind of Christ."

This is saying that if we have Christ in our lives, and the indwelling of the Holy Spirit, and are in the Word of God, we have the mind of Christ in us, and we are to use that Mind of Christ to evaluate all that we do. We are not to use the world's standards, but we are to use Christ's standards, and we are to think like Him and agree with Him on matters.

Paul, in 2 Cor. 5:16 says this, "There from now on we recognize no man according to the flesh; even though we have known Christ according to the flesh, yet now we know Him thus no longer."

Paul goes on to explain about being a new creation in Christ Jesus. Paul says that he no longer knows anyone according to the flesh. The Greek word used for know is that he no longer looks at people with his natural eyes, nor does he look on people according to his natural senses.

This is what we do when we pick pastors and people for ministry by their age, appearance, statistics, etc. Paul would refute the reasoning behind these ways of viewing or picking people.

If we were to look at age and appearance you would do well to think of Moses, and you can read about him in Exodus starting in the first chapter. He was hated by Israel in the beginning, and was wanted by Egypt for murder, and by the way was 80 years old when he started his ministry, and was slow of speech and had to take Aaron with him, but the truth of the matter was he was God's man to lead Israel.

What about Paul, who we read his story in Acts chapter 9. Here is a man that was one of the most educated men in Israel during his day. He was headed to be the youngest member of the Sanhedrin in the history of Israel. We find him in Acts chapter 9 breathing threats of murder against the disciples of Christ.

This is after he gave approval to the stoning of Steven. After his conversion on the road to Damascus, not only did the Jews not like him, but some of the church did not like him as well. Some had even followed him around trying to discredit him. He wasn't one for appearances. He had even described himself as not speaking well in public.

God not only used Paul to start many of the churches in Asia Minor, but Paul had pastored a number of them, and God used him to write two thirds of the New Testament. So it wasn't the standards that we pick today that was used to choose Paul.

Paul speaks in terms of a discernment that we are to have that is according to a new way of life. He looks for evidence of the Spirit at work in their lives. We know this evidence as "fruits of the Spirit", and evidence of the giftings of the office of pastor.

Paul completely rejects the way the world picks their leaders, and wants us to begin to practice the spiritual life that Jesus has given to us through the indwelling of the Holy Spirit.

The truth of the matter is that we don't do this because it isn't as easy to perceive the gifts of the spirit, and many times those involved are not aware of the things they are to look for. And most often when people are placed on the pastor search committee they are not trained and equipped to do so.

Pastors are not pastors because they fill the pulpit. Pastors are pastors because they have been gifted with the gifts of the pastorate. Pastors are to teach, preach, and equip the saints for the work of ministry. They are to lead their congregations into maturity in Christ.

Unfortunately, today many that are in the pulpit are philosophers and not pastors. They are there to make people feel good about themselves and do little to equip or maturity.

The whole idea behind maturing in the faith is so that we are not thrown here and there by every wind of doctrine that comes along. That is not what is going on today. In fact the church has so many new doctrines that it is divided against itself.

Paul explained to Timothy in 2 Timothy 4:3-4, "For the time will come when they will not tolerate sound doctrine, but according to their own desires, will they accumulate teachers for themselves because they have an itch to hear something new."

If we were to translate the Greek language with respect to tolerate sound doctrine it means this, they will not hold to, or stand erect to doctrine that is healthy. He says that they will want to hear things that make them feel good, or they will want something new and different.

This is scary. Are we there? Are we willing to hold to, or stand erect to healthy doctrine, or are we looking for something new? Unfortunately we are in many cases looking for something new. We are not holding to healthy doctrine.

This is a really bad time to do these things. We are, as never before, closer to our Lord's return than we have ever been, and yet we find that statistics show more and more evangelical Christians do not believe in the resurrection of the saints. They are hiring pastors according to their age, appearance, and statistics.

It is time to get back to the foundation of our Christian beliefs and stop looking for something new. We do not have the truth Jesus taught us down; why should we be looking for something new? We need to get our eyes back on the author and finisher of our faith Jesus Christ.

www.ingramcontent.com/pod-product-compliance
Ingram Content Group UK Ltd.
Pitfield, Milton Keynes, MK11 3LW, UK
UKHW022215230426
12048UKWH00016BA/865